JEREMY TAYLOR

All Kicking Off
in South Africa

CORNELSEN
ENGLISH
LIBRARY

CORNELSEN **ENGLISH** LIBRARY

Jeremy Taylor: *All Kicking Off in South Africa*

Verlagsredaktion
Michael Dunkel; Jutta Seuren

Umschlaggestaltung
hawemannundmosch, Konzeption und Gestaltung, Berlin

Bildquellen
Titelbild: Shutterstock.com/Rawpixel.com; Emoticon S. 5 u. 85: Shutterstock.com/
Perfect icons; Karte S. 126/127: Carlos Borrell Eiköter

Layout & technische Umsetzung
Yvonne Thron (designcollective), Berlin

*The author would like to thank Namhla Mphelo at the South African Football
Association, Tyrone Gunnie at the South African Embassy in London and Debbie
Grüber, a South African teacher trainer.*

www. cornelsen.de

1. Auflage, 1. Druck 2020

Alle Drucke dieser Auflage sind inhaltlich unverändert und können
im Unterricht nebeneinander verwendet werden.

Druck: H. Heenemann, Berlin

ISBN 978-3-06-036236-3

PEFC zertifiziert
Dieses Produkt stammt aus nachhaltig
bewirtschafteten Wäldern und kontrollierten
Quellen.

www.pefc.de

PEFC/04-31-1156

Contents

Chapter One

15 January 2020: Soweto,
South Africa

Tommy Gilmour

Leave the country – or Amahle will never walk again.

I used to like text messages. I prefer them to calling someone. Who knows what they might be doing? A quick text:

5   Football in the park @4?

And five minutes later I'd get a reply.

Sure. And this time we'll win. ☺

But this text was different, very different. It was from the people who were holding Amahle. I was being threatened, but nothing like the way Amahle was being threatened. I had a decision to make: leave the country and save my own skin, or stay and try to save Amahle. Realistically, I didn't have a chance. But more importantly, this was personal, and I knew that I didn't have a choice.

Ms Manifold

The word I would use for Tommy is 'original'. I think a lot
of young people feel that they have to fit in with their classmates: wear the same clothes, listen to the same music,
support the same limited number of football teams. Not
5 Tommy. When all the other boys were wearing baggy
trousers, Tommy wore tight jeans. When all his classmates
were listening to Ed Sheeran, Tommy was listening to
Radiohead, Schubert and Joni Mitchell (I'm surprised anyone under 25 has heard of Joni Mitchell, let alone enjoys
10 listening to her music). And while Tommy was mad about
football, he was always playing it, rather than talking about
the top teams or Bristol Rovers, our local club. There was
also a melancholy side to Tommy. Sometimes I would see
him in class, staring into space, a million miles away
15 from Waterbridge. Where was he? What was he thinking
about?

I should introduce myself. I'm Phillipa Manifold, or
Manni as my friends and some of the students call me. I'm
head of the sixth form at Waterbridge High School in
20 Bristol. I teach A level and GCSE biology and general science
in the lower years. We have some difficult students who
have problems or come from difficult homes – but on the
whole, we are a 'desirable' school in a 'desirable' area. I know
quite a few parents who have moved to the area so that
25 their children can go to Waterbridge.

But back to Tommy. While I admired Tommy for his in-
dividuality, I have to say he was a pain in the neck to have in

my class. Some days he wouldn't say a thing and it seemed that there was a black cloud hanging over him. But there were other times when he had an idea that he wanted to test out. Most students wanted to know enough biology so that they could get a good A level result and get a place at university. Not Tommy. While I was confident that he would get a good grade, it didn't stop him going off on tangents in the blink of an eye. I remember one lesson I was explaining about the different enzymes that break down our food in the digestive system. Out of the corner of my eye I could see that Tommy's brain was working hard. I tried to continue, but I knew that I would soon have a question from Tommy.

"So while there are enzymes in our saliva which start the process of digestion, the main …"

I could see Tommy's mop of blond hair moving around as he slowly raised his thin arm.

"The main digestive processes begin …"

It was no good. I knew I couldn't continue with Tommy's question unanswered.

"Yes, Tommy?"

"Manni, if all these enzymes in our gut break down the fats, sugars, proteins and so on, wouldn't it be possible to find a drug that could block the enzymes that break down sugars and fats, so we could all eat as much chocolate and full-fat ice cream as we want to, and the sugars and fats would just pass straight through us?"

It was a good question and if I meet a nutritional scientist, I'll definitely ask them about Tommy's idea. But when we are just a few months away from the exam, I want my students to know all the basics and not worry too much about new drugs.

Amahle Nyembezi

I can see out of the window. My right hand is chained to a
massive old cooker, but I can see the tops of trees. When
they took me, they put a bag over my head and put me in
the back of a car. It's hard to say how far they took me,
but I'm pretty sure I'm still in Soweto. But as I'm not on
the ground floor, I think I might be in Diepkloof, where the
richer people live. I remember we played a football match
here once.

I can move about three metres around the cooker. A boy,
maybe about six years old, brings me food and water twice
a day. I try to engage him in conversation, but I'm sure he's
been told not to say anything to me. There's no bed here, I
just sleep on the floor with my hoodie as a pillow. I have a
bucket which is my toilet.

I have to admit, I'm scared. Life is cheap here in Soweto;
people get killed every day. Is that their plan? So why haven't
they killed me? They can't be waiting for a ransom; my family haven't got more than a few thousand rand, and they
struggle to pay the rent each month.

What will Tommy be thinking? And what about Kaya?
I've been here for two days now. I was going to have a drink
with Tommy on the 15th. He knows I'm a reliable girl. If I
couldn't meet up for some reason, I'd send him a text. That
means he knows I'm missing now, but there's nothing he can
do about it.

Maybe they think they can get some money from Tommy.
As he's white and English, they probably think that he's

made of money, but that's not true. I know the school doesn't pay him that well, and he spends a lot of time in Soweto helping the local boys – I think that's why I love him. He's one of the few people I know, black or white, that does something because he believes in it, not just for the money.

Will I ever see him again? Will we ever practise our curling free kicks together again? I really do miss him.

21 October 2018: Waterbridge School,
Bristol, England

Ms Manifold

Last week I had to interview the members of the sixth form and offer them careers advice and also try to find courses that would suit whatever they wanted to do. I've done it for a few years now and I can usually tell what people are best suited to.

"So, Jessie, what are you hoping to do after A levels?"

"A degree in biochemistry at Exeter and then a PhD, probably in drug research," replied a super-confident Jessie.

"Sounds like you've got it all planned out."

"I have, Miss."

"So you don't need my help today. You've got all the information about applying to university?"

"I've already applied."

"That's good. Let's hope they make you a good offer."

"They already did. They made me an unconditional offer."

"Well, that's brilliant. Congratulations, Jessie."

"Thank you, Miss."

Other students were not quite so well-organised.

"So, Alfie, what are you hoping to do after A levels?"

"Dunno, Miss."

"Well, do you want to go to university, or would you rather do a more practical course, perhaps combined with work, accountancy or something like that?"

"Dunno, Miss."

"What about an apprenticeship? You could learn practical skills on the job and get some qualifications."

"Dunno, Miss."

If there are any employers out there looking for someone who is really good at saying 'Dunno, Miss', then Alfie Harrison is definitely the person you're looking for.

Then there was Tommy.

"So, Tommy, what are you hoping to do after A levels?"

"I haven't decided yet, and of course it will depend on what grades I get at A level, but I was thinking either cosmology, forestry or ..."

"Or what?"

"Or football. I know it's tough out there and I'm 18 already and I haven't been spotted by any of the big clubs."

"Yet," I added, always good to encourage a growth mindset in students.

"True, not yet. But what do you think, Manni? What do *you* think I should do?"

That was a very good question. What was it that Ophelia said in *Hamlet*? 'We know what we are, but know not what we may be.' I wasn't really sure what Tommy was, and I definitely had no idea what Tommy would be in the future. I couldn't give him an Alfie Harrison answer, 'Dunno, Tommy.' I had to say something.

"Have you thought about a gap year?"

"A year backpacking around South East Asia with thousands of other eighteen-year-olds?"

"You wouldn't have to go backpacking. There are lots of other possibilities."

"Like what?" asked Tommy.

"Give me a couple of days and I'll get back to you with some ideas," I said, which is what people say when they really haven't got a clue.

Tommy smiled. I'm pretty sure he knew I didn't have a clue. "Okay, see you in a couple of days, Manni."

Chapter Two

23 October 2018: Waterbridge School,
Bristol, England

Tommy

"South Africa?"

Manni nodded. "I think it would be … interesting."

"What do you mean by 'interesting'?"

"You're a bright young man, Tommy. You've got a very
active brain, and it needs to be stimulated. As you said,
backpacking round South East Asia or WOOFing in New
Zealand is not for you. This could be more of a challenge."

I looked through the information that she had printed
out for me. Ten months in South Africa as a football coach
in a multi-racial school in Johannesburg, all expenses
paid and a two-week holiday at the end of it – as well as all
school holidays.

"Is Johannesburg the capital of South Africa?"

Manni smiled. "I have to admit, I thought it was, but I
checked. It's by far the biggest city with nine million people,
but South Africa actually has three capitals: Pretoria,
Bloemfontein and Cape Town."

Wow, I'd never even heard of Bloemfontein before. I
clearly had a lot to learn about South Africa. What did I
know? I knew that there was apartheid, that disgusting
ideology where the white minority ruled over the black
majority. Thankfully that ended in the 1990s. I knew there
was an amazing man called Nelson Mandela who was in
prison for ages for his political beliefs and then came out

and said, 'Okay guys, let's all be friends and live in a rainbow nation.' I knew they had national parks with some fantastic animals. I knew they liked their sport, in particular rugby and cricket. What about football? Everybody loves football, don't they?

"I think you'd be great there. You could do a lot of good and you'd learn a lot – things that you can't learn at school."

I appreciated being treated as an intelligent adult by Manni. Sadly, not all teachers were like her. I told her I'd think about it for a couple of days, but I could see a year in South Africa would be interesting, stimulating and challenging. It would be a chance to meet people very different from my classmates at Waterbridge. It might even help me to think less about certain things.

23 October 2018: Tommy's home,
Bristol, England

Wendy Gilmour (Tommy's mum)

"South Africa? Are you nuts?"

I knew that Tommy wasn't like other eighteen-year-olds, but where did he get such a crazy idea from? I couldn't believe that he was even thinking of going to South Africa. I know young people these days don't watch the news on TV, but he must have heard some of the stories from South Africa.

"It simply isn't safe, Tommy! There are hundreds, thousands of road accidents in South Africa every year."

Why didn't he just want to go backpacking around South East Asia like normal gap-year students? He could have all sorts of adventures there – I know, I did the same thing twenty years ago. I broke my leg when I fell off a motorbike in Vietnam. I was on the back of a motorbike ridden by my boyfriend at the time. I had no idea he'd never ridden a motorbike before. Or WOOFing – that's Working On an Organic Farm. My niece went WOOFing in Australia. She had a brilliant time.

"And crime! I don't know what the crime rate is now, but I bet it's massive!"

I had my bag stolen at Angkor Wat. The enterprising thief snatched it from my shoulder and scampered up a tree. We watched as he threw down my wallet, passport and box of tampons before finding a banana at the bottom of the bag. He peeled and ate it while looking at me and my boyfriend picking up my belongings from the ground below him which, for some reason, he found to be hilarious. In case you haven't realised, the thief was a monkey – watch out for them.

"And what about diseases? Hepatitis, tuberculosis, HIV ..."

A few years ago, my husband bought me a coat – it was the most waterproof coat I have ever owned. You could pour water on it, and the water would just run off, leaving the coat completely dry. The same was true with my efforts to persuade Tommy not to go to South Africa. The more reasons I showered him with, the faster they ran off and formed a puddle on the floor. I love Tommy, but unfortunately he has got my gene for stubbornness. It was pretty clear that there was no way of stopping him doing something that he really wanted to do.

Chapter Three

*27 October 2018: Notting Hill
Recruitment Programme Centre,
London, England*

Major Edward Goodfellow (retired)

"Been to South Africa before, have you, Thomas?"

"No, I can't say I have."

"Beautiful place. You'll have a splendid time there. Absolutely splendid."

5   These selection days are a bit of a joke. We'll take pretty much anyone who is willing to spend ten months away from home, working for next to nothing. My cousin, Jennifer, runs a school in Joburg and she relies on me and my organisation to get support staff for the school, teaching assist-

10 ants and in the case of Thomas Gilmour, a sports coach.

She sent me a presentation which I show to all prospective candidates. Even the ones who seem unsure at first are won over pretty quickly.

"Now this, Thomas, is the Kruger National Park, home to

15 lots of fantastic animals which I hope you'll shoot …"

I always pause there, and normally there will be a look of surprise or horror on the young face in front of me, but with Thomas there was neither. It would take more than one of my little jokes to rattle him. I continued.

20 "… with your camera of course. Ha ha."

He didn't laugh with me.

I clicked through the remaining slides. A lovely shot of Table Mountain – true, it's in Cape Town, about 800 miles from where he would be working, but it looks great and he might get the chance to travel down there. Thomas sat
5 impassively as I showed him photos of typical food he's likely to find in South Africa. Normally, candidates turn up their noses at the boerewors sausages. I think they're made from recycled hiking boots – and definitely taste like it. Even the disgusting mix of chicken heads and feet known
10 as 'walkie-talkie' didn't raise a smile from young Thomas Gilmour.

"Ever considered a career in the army, Thomas?"

"I've considered it, yes."

"Good man. The army could do with fellows like you."

4 November 2018: Tommy's home,
Bristol, England

Tommy

15 I had never realised that people like Major Edward Goodfellow actually existed. He's one of those people who are clearly devastated by the fact that Britain no longer rules the world. No one I have ever met before uses phrases like 'absolutely splendid'. Such phrases seem to belong in
20 the 1940s. I presume he is one of those people who went to public school and then to the elite military training college, Sandhurst, and then off to shout at young recruits who leave school at 16.

Towards the end of the interview, he asked me if I'd
25 considered a career in the army, and I said yes which was

the honest answer. I didn't tell him that I thought about it for about ten seconds. I realise that there is a role for soldiers in the world, but it's not for me at all.

I should say that I got an email saying that I've been accepted on the programme and I'll be flying out at the end of August next year. We have a week of 'induction' and then we get to start work in early September. There are four of us going to South Africa. As you know, I'm going to Johannesburg – or Joburg as people call it. Joe and Jack, twins from Leicester, are going to Bloemfontein, and an enthusiastic girl called Olivia will be working in Cape Town. I've been doing a bit of research, and it seems that she's the lucky one as Cape Town looks beautiful.

We've set up a messaging group online so that we can keep in touch and pass on advice about things to take, vaccinations we'll need and places we can visit and stuff like that. I have to admit that I'm feeling pretty excited about South Africa; I'm really glad that Manni told me about it.

5 November 2018: Epsom,
Surrey, England

Olivia Johnston

"Hi, guys! Great to meet you! I'm Olivia! As you can probably tell, I'm originally from Sydney, Australia, but I've spent the last five years in Epsom in Surrey."

I had them up on my screen, Jack and Joe, the twins. Nice-looking guys! Not that I'm looking for anyone at the moment of course. I'll be doing my A levels and then a year in South Africa. But I am really excited about going.

"Hi, I'm Jack," said Jack, the twin with short hair.

"And I'm Joe," said Joe, the twin with long hair.

"Hi, Jack! Hi, Joe!" I waved at the camera. The twins waved back.

"Nice to meet you, Olivia," said Jack.

"Hi!" said Joe.

Then Tommy joined our group.

"Hello, I'm Tommy," he said.

"We were just saying hi," I said to Tommy. "That's Jack with the short hair, Joe with the long hair – and I'm Olivia."

Tommy waved at the camera and smiled. "Hi, guys! I think we're going to have a pretty special time in South Africa."

We definitely were. Tommy seemed to be a very nice guy – cute as well. Shame that he'll be in Johannesburg – I checked online and it is about 1,400 kilometres away from Cape Town, but I also checked that there are plenty of cheap flights, so I could hop up and see Tommy, or he could come down and see me. Jack and Joe are nice enough guys, but I've had a look at Bloemfontein, and apart from a couple of nice buildings it looks pretty dull. A bit like Canberra in Australia – stuck in the middle of the country, but who actually wants to live there? No, I'm sure Cape Town and Johannesburg – or Joburg as Tommy called it – are the best places to be. I am a big fan of music, and apparently there are loads of music clubs where you can go and hear some amazing sounds. Yes, by this time next year I'll have finished my A levels and I might be sitting in a music bar somewhere in South Africa with Tommy Gilmour; that sounds pretty good to me.

Chapter Four

27 August 2019: Heathrow Airport,
London, England

Tommy

"Tommy Gilmour!"

I'm not much of a hugger, but I found myself being hugged by Olivia Johnston. "It's so good to, like, finally meet you!"

"You, too, Olivia," I said once she'd finally let go of me. "So this is it. We're finally off."

"I can't wait! It's going to be, like, brilliant! The trip of a lifetime!"

It was interesting listening to Olivia. Her accent was a mix of Australian and some posh home counties British English, and she overused the word 'like'. She was born in Australia but then came over to the UK when she was 13. Her mum is an architect, and apparently London is the place to be if you're good at designing offices.

"Fancy some scroggin?"

"Er, what's scroggin?"

"It's what we Australians call trail mix. I made it myself last night."

Olivia held out a bag full of nuts and dried fruit, and I took a handful. It was pretty good.

"Have you tried pap yet?" asked Olivia with a mouthful of scroggin.

I had heard the name, but I couldn't quite place it. "Can you remind me what it is?"

"It's a kind of, like, porridge made with maize."

"I quite like porridge."

"Me too, I love it, but I can't say the same for pap. I made some last week using a South African recipe I found online. On its own it's, like, really bland, but I put together a kind of, like, ratatouille and that made it edible. Apparently in South Africa, some people eat it, like, three times a day! I read that ..."

"Jack! Joe! We're over here!"

We were joined by Jack and Joe who had just come down on the coach from Leicester. Handshakes from me and hugs from Olivia. The team was ready.

"The coach broke down on the motorway. We thought we were going to miss the flight," said Jack.

"But luckily a replacement bus arrived after 20 minutes," explained Joe.

"Well it's great you're here now," said Olivia. "Would you like some scroggin?"

They took a handful each, and we made our way over to the check-in counters. We still had a couple of hours before our flight, so it was a good opportunity for us to get to know each other. Jack and Joe seem like chilled guys, a bit quiet, but perhaps that was in contrast with Olivia. She's nice and friendly, but her overuse of the word 'like' is a bit annoying. Olivia seems to use it in almost every sentence.

Jack Sterling

"Welcome to South Africa! My name is Jennifer Goodfellow.
I'll be your coordinator in South Africa."

So we are finally here after an eleven-hour flight, the
longest flight I've ever taken. We took off at 7.05 last night
and arrived at 7.05 in the morning local time. South Africa
is an hour ahead of Britain, the same as most of Europe. Of
course, we were in economy, and Joe and I were lucky enough
to have a window seat – well *he* had a window seat, but I
spent most of my time leaning over him to watch the world
beneath us. I've only flown three times before, so this was
pretty special. It was getting dark as we passed over the
Mediterranean and it was a strange feeling looking down
and seeing the coast of Africa; according to the map on the
little screen it was Algeria.

You're probably aware that Africa is huge, but what I
hadn't realised was how empty it is. When you fly over
Europe at night, then you can see loads of lights every-
where. Flying over Africa, you can fly for ages without seeing
a single light. Okay, you're unlikely to be able to see a single
light, but I was surprised not to see more towns and cities.

"Maybe there *are* people down there, but they don't use
loads of electricity at night," said Joe. "We could learn a
lesson or two from them."

Fair point; he's a smart cookie my brother.

People often say bad things about airline food, but the
meal we had was fine. It can't be easy serving top quality
food when you're ten kilometres up in the air. After the

meal, I got up to go to the loo and passed Olivia and Tommy on the way. They had aisle seats, so they couldn't look out the window. I heard Olivia telling Tommy about some of the flights she's been on.

5 "There was one time when we were coming back from Australia, and the plane just dropped for, like, five thousand metres. I thought I was going to, like, die."

How can you 'like die'? Surely you either die, or you survive.

29 August 2019: teachers' room, St George's School,
Johannesburg, South Africa

Jennifer Goodfellow

10 "So, good morning, everyone. Has anyone seen Olivia?"

"She wasn't at breakfast," said Tommy. "She's in the room next to mine, shall I ..."

"Sorry I'm late! I slept, like, really deeply, you see. I didn't sleep very well on the plane and I think I might be suffering 15 from, like, jet lag."

As there is only an hour difference between the UK and South Africa that seems unlikely, but I smiled at Olivia and she smiled back. That made up the full team this year, just four.

20 She was just in time to see my slide show and film of a potted history of South Africa. I've done this 15 times now and I'm pretty bored with it, but they get the basic message: South Africa in 2019 is a complex place.

"Hope you enjoyed the film, guys. That should fill you in 25 on some of the history that you might not have studied in

England. If you have any questions, you can ask me or any of the teachers, you'll be working with in the coming year. Please be aware that our history is a touchy subject for many teachers, so please tread carefully."

5   I have to say we get quite a few people coming here from England who think that we are not aware that apartheid was unfair and that everyone should be treated equally and feel that every white South African is guilty. They don't get how complicated things are here. They seem to think that there 10 is a quick fix to the complex problems in the country: can I just snap my fingers so that all black South Africans will be qualified to work as architects, scientists and top civil servants? Can I wave my magic wand so that every South African has electricity and water available at home? Shall I 15 give the magic money tree a good shake so that everyone can get a well-paid job? Dream on, guys, it's not that easy.

    "What we can do here at St George's, and our sister schools in Cape Town and Bloemfontein, is to bring up young people in South Africa to believe in three things: 20 honesty, integrity and justice – HIJ as I call them. You can be brilliant at trigonometry, amazing at chemical equations or a talented cricket player, but this country will not get anywhere if people don't believe in HIJ. Okay, enough of the heavy stuff. After lunch you'll be going with one of 25 our drivers, King, to Soweto. Now I'm sure you've all heard of Soweto before. The 1976 Soweto uprising usually makes it into the history books around the world, but let me tell you, things have changed a lot since then. Soweto even has Diepkloof, the Beverley Hills of Soweto if you will.

30   "Anyway, King will look after you. It's pretty safe during the day, but I strongly recommend you don't go there after

dark. There are some pretty unsavoury characters around, and you really don't want to mess with the South African underworld. And, on that happy note, I think it's time for some lunch."

Tommy

5 Olivia was right. Pap is not great, but as I was going to be here for a year, it was something I knew I had to get used to. In the cafeteria it was served with a kind of tomato-flavoured gravy. It made my mum's cooking taste pretty good which is saying something. There were just the four of us in
10 the cafeteria as there was still a week before school started.

"So what did you think of the film?" asked Olivia.

"It was interesting to see in film what I'd read about in books," said Jack. "The people we'll be working with actually lived through some of the events. Mandela was released in
15 1990, so people who are about forty or older will remember it."

"It was touching to see the joy on the faces of the people when he was released. They realised that this was the beginning of something new," said Joe.

20 "And what about the white South Africans?" asked Olivia. "I'm sure there were some that were like, 'Let's get out of here! There's no way we can live with a black president.'"

For me, that's what made Nelson Mandela such an incredible man. He was in prison for 27 years and then he comes out and says, 'Okay everybody, let's be friends.' What he did was remarkable.

"Hello, my name's King. I'll be your guide today."

King was only a couple of years older than us and sat
5 down to have a coffee with us in the cafeteria. He asked about our first impressions of South Africa and what we already knew about Soweto. We had all read about the history of Soweto and seen various clips on the internet and on the film that Jennifer showed us this morning, but I
10 was sure that the reality would be very different.

"School has asked me to tell you that Soweto is generally safe during the day, but you should stay with me at all times and not go wandering off," said King. "So, that said, let's meet at one o'clock at the front of the school, and I'll show you
15 where I grew up."

29 August 2019: Soweto,
South Africa

Kungawo Nyembezi (King)

Only four of them this year. I joined the school five years ago, and there were 17 enthusiastic young people from Britain, all coming to enjoy a year in South Africa. Since then, the numbers have gone down. South Africa is a great country,
20 but I realise it is not everyone's cup of tea. It's a tough place, and for many people life is a real struggle. There are parts of Soweto that I wouldn't want to go, day or night, but on the whole, people are friendly. As long as you don't wander around with a ten-thousand-dollar camera hanging around
25 your neck, you'll be fine. Oh, and perhaps it's not a good idea

to try and move in on someone else's territory in the drug world. Those guys would definitely kill you and ask questions later.

"So guys, this is Soweto. Do you know where the name comes from?"

"It's the South Western Townships. So-we-to," said Joe.

"Good to hear you've done your homework, Joe. Now for the rest of you, I could spend an hour or two telling you about the history of Soweto, but I don't want to bore you. I want you to experience the real Soweto as it is today. We can't forget the past, but we also have to look forward. Let's build on what we have."

The four of them were listening attentively. The girl, Olivia, sat in the front of the minibus next to me. She had a pretty nice camera and was taking more shots than I took in the first 15 years of my life. I've never been to Europe, but I doubt if there is anywhere like Soweto there.

The boys in the back took some photos with their phones. I noticed that the blond boy, Tommy, had a pretty cheap phone with a large crack across the front – a crack that had the shape of a smile. Even my phone was better than his. It got me thinking, did he have a cheap phone with him because he thought a more expensive phone might get stolen? Or perhaps he was a fan of Fridays for Future, so he didn't believe in upgrading his mobile every ten minutes. While the others had lots of questions about Soweto and its most famous resident, Nelson Mandela, Tommy remained pretty quiet. Was he bored? He definitely looked sad. What was he doing in South Africa?

"This area looks different from Diepkloof. Are the people, like, poorer here?" asked Olivia.

"This is Orlando, Soweto. It's a little bit different from Orlando, Florida. There are no theme parks here, but for those of you interested in history, there is an important museum here. Are you familiar with a boy called Hector Pieterson?"

Once again, it was Joe that had the answer. He knew all about Hector and his tragically short life. After a sombre visit to the Hector Pieterson Museum, Olivia had a question, or rather a comment. "What I don't get is that the white South Africans must have known what was going on. Surely, when that kind of thing happens, people would complain, there would be, like, demonstrations against the police. The policemen who shot Hector should have been, like, arrested and sent to prison."

It is easy to see Olivia as very naive, but her view is common. If you've always lived in a functioning democracy, it is very difficult to understand why you can't just write to the newspaper, go and talk to the police or organise a demonstration. As anyone who has lived in a brutally oppressive regime will know, it takes a huge amount of courage to stand up against the regime; the kind of courage that normal people don't have. Fortunately, South Africa has had some very brave people who were willing to confront the regime, to try to right the wrongs. Many of them, like Hector Pieterson, paid for it with their lives.

Nelson Mandela's home was, as usual, very popular. He is one of two or three South Africans that people from other countries have heard of. Olivia snapped away with her expensive camera, even asking me to take her photo with the boys.

The place where I grew up is not far from Mandela's house. My mum still lives there with my three sisters and two brothers. She does a great job feeding them all, and I give her what I can from the money I get from St George's.

Chapter Five

29 August 2019: Orlando,
Soweto, South Africa

Amahle

I saw my brother in the minibus – the one he drives when he comes to Soweto, not the big fancy one with 'St George's' written on the side, but an old pale blue one, one that wouldn't stand out in Soweto. I was training my team when I saw his minibus. There was a ball close to my feet, so I ran up and kicked it. The ball curled through the air and hit the windscreen of his minibus. Bingo!

"*Sawubona,* Kungawo!" I called. "*Unjani?*"

"*Sawubona,*" he replied. "I'm *sharp.* We're just taking a look around Soweto. These guys arrived from England yesterday." And speaking to the four people in the minibus, he introduced me, "This is my sister, Amahle."

"Hi, Amahle!" said an excitable girl with long blonde hair. "I'm Olivia. Lovely to meet you! Your brother's an awesome guide. He knows, like, everything about Soweto!"

"Hello, Olivia. Welcome to Soweto."

"That was an impressive curl on the ball," said the boy with the blond hair in the back. "Do you play in a team?"

"I play for the Orlando Ladies Football Club – and train the youth team as well."

I was happy to see my brother, but the girls were waiting for me on the field. I ran and picked up the ball that I had kicked against his windscreen and, giving them all a quick wave, I ran back to the girls on the field.

As we practised sprinting up and down the field, I thought about the boy with the blond hair. I get plenty of compliments from boys, but this one had complimented me on my football skills and had shown interest in me not as a woman, but as a sportswoman; that was pretty rare.

30 August 2019: school gymnasium,
St George's School, Johannesburg, South Africa

Tommy

"We've got lots of basketballs in this cupboard here, volley-balls over there. Nets for volleyball are kept here – and I'll show you how to put them up later." Graeme Logan, head of sports at St George's, was filling me in and showing me the ropes – literally – in the school gymnasium. They had a lot of equipment, more than we had at Waterbridge, and it looked like it was well used.

"Some of the boys like basketball, but the big sports at St George's, in fact all over South Africa, are football and rugby," said Graeme. "You've probably picked up that we are sports mad. Our cricket team is doing pretty well, our rugby team won the World Cup and our football team is getting better every year."

I'd read about sport in South Africa and I was secretly supporting them in the Rugby World Cup in 2018. It was brilliant that they won and it was wonderful to hear about the captain, Siya Kolisi, who grew up in a township outside Port Elizabeth.

While I enjoyed the Rugby World Cup, I never played it at school and I was quite nervous about teaching it at

St George's. Football was my game, and I was very familiar with the national team, Bafana Bafana as they are known. I knew that for some South Africans, football was a way out of poverty. There were quite a few players in top European clubs who were from townships like Soweto. Racism in all areas of life is still a problem, but things are getting much better in football. 99% of managers don't care about the colour of your skin.

That made me think about the girl we met in Soweto, King's sister, Amahle I think her name was.

One thing I noticed when Amahle was talking to her brother was that they were greeting each other in Zulu but then switching to English. When she addressed him, I'm sure she called him Kungawo rather than King. I asked him about it afterwards, and he explained that Jennifer Goodfellow started calling him King as she found Kungawo difficult to remember. Personally, I think someone's name is important, and a name like Kungawo is not particularly difficult. I vowed to call him Kungawo whenever we met.

18 September 2019: Jennifer
Goodfellow's office, St George's School,
Johannesburg, South Africa

Graeme Logan

"Looking at the positives, Tommy is a good lad, much better than the boy we had last year. He's a very good football player, and the boys on the football team seem to be happy with him."

"And the negatives?" asked Jennifer.

"Well, his rugby skills are non-existent. My dog plays rugby better than Tommy. I watched him training with the younger boys, and they were explaining the rules to him!"

"Anything else?"

What could I tell Jennifer? There *was* something else, but it was very difficult to put my finger on. Tommy turned up on time, he was polite with me, the other members of staff and with the boys. But there was something missing. He was undoubtedly a great football player, much better than me, but I get the feeling that his heart is not in the job. Sometimes I'm sitting next to him having a coffee and I notice that he is miles away with his thoughts. I don't know him well enough to ask about his home life, and if you ask him how things are, he always replies *'sharp'*.

"No, that's it at the moment. I'll take over his rugby training and he can do my hours on the football field, I think that'll work."

"Good to hear it, Graeme. You know how the parents are. They're paying a lot of money for their boys to come to St George's. We can't let them down."

Chapter Six

26 September 2019: St George's School,
Johannesburg, South Africa

Tommy

Yesterday was an interesting day. I was keen to go back to Orlando because I feel that Soweto is a real place, with real people leading tough but very real lives. Life in central Joburg and particularly life at St George's just doesn't seem right –
5 I'm living in a bubble here. I mean most of the kids are okay. There are some cheeky ones, some lazy ones and some that just want to make your life as difficult as possible.

So while I was working hard to maintain the privilege of the privileged, I'm certain that it is not what I want to do,
10 even in my short time here in South Africa. I suppose I'll have to continue my work at St George's, but I hope I can find some more work, real work, in Orlando – and I think I know someone who might be able to help.

After school yesterday, I took a taxi to Orlando. When I
15 say taxi, you probably imagine a comfortable car with a driver who has satnav. South African taxis are a little different, and riding in one is a real experience. I went to the Bree taxi rank – home to hundreds of minibuses known as taxis. You don't ride alone in a South African taxi; you are
20 squeezed in with another 200 passengers. I found out that the drivers have to rent their minibuses, so they work 25 hours a day to pay the rent, pay for the petrol and also earn enough money to support a family.

The 25-minute taxi ride was not the most comfortable journey I've had, but I got to Orlando which is where I wanted to be. I got a boerewors from one of the stands near the place where the taxi stopped. They have a lot more flavour than English sausages, but I'm not sure I want to know what is inside them.

"Excuse me," I said to the guy selling the boerewors. "I'm looking for a girl called Amahle. She plays football."

The man shook his head. I don't know if he didn't understand me or if he didn't know Amahle. I smiled at him and left. I strolled down the street, looking at the various shops and restaurants. A silver BMW with tinted windows pulled up at the kerb. The driver jumped out and opened the back door. A short man with gold chains around his neck got out and walked into a restaurant as though he owned the place – perhaps he did. There were definitely some people here who had money.

After five minutes, I saw a sports shop. There was a simple display of footballs and a large yellow South African football shirt in the window. I was confident this was the right place to ask about Amahle. A small bell tinkled as I entered.

"Can I help you?" The woman behind the counter was also wearing a large yellow football shirt and had a baby resting on her hip.

"Um, yes, I think you can. I'm looking for a woman. She's a footballer and she trains girls. Her name is Amahle."

It was clear that the woman knew Amahle, but it was also clear she was pretty suspicious of me. I suppose she had every right to be suspicious.

"And why might you be interested in this woman?"

"I want to help her, and I'd like to train some boys from Soweto. I'm a football coach from England."

She stared at me for a while and then picked up her mobile and spoke in a language I didn't know. Who was she calling? The police? Some guys to come and teach me a lesson? Why hadn't I simply asked Kungawo to give me Amahle's number?

"Wait here," she said calmly.

I have to admit, I was nervous. I hadn't told anyone where I was going, and this woman was not the friendliest person in the world. I looked through the basket of footballs she had and picked out a good one.

"I'll take this one, please."

Just as the woman was giving me my change, I heard the tinkle of the shop door. I turned slowly, not knowing what to expect. In front of me stood two girls in tracksuits, both of them about eleven.

"You want to meet Amahle?" asked the taller one.

"Yes, yes I do," I replied.

"Come with us."

I turned to the shopkeeper. *"Ngiyabonga."*

"Sho," she replied with, I think, a very small smile on her face.

Amahle

I was busy training with the girls when my phone rang. It
was Mrs Khumalo from the sports shop on Vilakazi Street.
She said there was a man looking for me and she was
concerned. I shared her concern – there are some strange
5   people in Soweto, and I'd rather keep away from them if
possible. I asked for a description of the man. She told me
he was white, had blond hair, was quite good-looking, and
said that he was into football.

It was clear it was the guy in Kungawo's minibus – but
10 what did he want with me? There was only one way to find
out. I sent two of my girls to Vilakazi Street to bring him back
to the playing field.

"*Sawubona,*" he said. "*Unjani?*"

"*Sharp,*" I replied, actually impressed that he'd bothered
15 to learn some Zulu.

"I'm Tommy Gilmour. I'd like to talk to you about football – about the possibility of training a group of boys."

"I thought you were already doing that at St George's."

"Well, I am, but I think the boys in Soweto need me more."

20 I could see he was sincere, and there were plenty of boys
who could benefit from some football coaching. "I finish
with the girls in half an hour. Can we meet after that?"

"Sure, do you mind if I watch you?"

"*Ayikho inkinga.*"

25 He sat and watched as I put the girls through their paces.
They were a great bunch of girls, and I had high hopes of
getting them into the national team. Most of the girls were

hoping to be talent spotted by a European coach, so naturally they had a question or two about the blond English guy who had turned up at our training session.

After training, I walked with Tommy to a coffee shop. We ordered coffees and sat at the window, watching the world go by. We talked *a lot* about football. He seemed surprised that I knew so much about European football. I told him about growing up in Soweto. He seemed genuinely interested, not just showing an interest in what I was saying because he wanted something extra.

He talked about his mum and a teacher called Manni. Strangely he didn't mention his dad at all. I wasn't sure if he was still alive. I was pretty sure he wasn't living with Tommy's mum, but I didn't know him well enough to ask.

We exchanged mobile numbers so we could stay in contact. I told him I'd try and get a group of boys together that he could train.

Tommy offered to pay for my coffee, but I was keen to pay my own way, so we went Dutch. I did accept his kind present though, a new football. Most of the footballs that I use with the girls are left over from the World Cup in South Africa back in 2010, so they are not in the best condition anymore. I walked with Tommy back to the taxi stop. When his taxi pulled up, I wasn't sure if we were going to shake hands or embrace, and we ended up doing both which was a bit awkward. Tommy's a special boy and I think he's going to do a lot of good for some of the boys of Soweto. I just hope he knows what he's doing.

Chapter Seven

17 October 2019: St George's School,
Johannesburg, South Africa

Tommy

"You've got to time your run perfectly. Half a second too early and you'll be offside. Half a second too late and the defender will be back there with you. Timing is everything. Now go out there and show me what I know you're capable
5   of."

It was not easy managing the under fifteens. They were at that difficult age, not yet adults but not really children either.

"Come on, St George's!" shouted Jennifer Goodfellow
10   from the touchline as the players ran out for the second half. "You can do it!"

Sadly, I didn't think the team could 'do it'. They seemed quite surprised to be 4–1 down at half time, and it was unlikely they would be able to score three goals in the second
15   half. Despite hours of training them in beating the offside trap, their hearts just weren't in it.

Which, to be honest, is not a surprise. My heart wasn't in it either. I did my hours, well, most of them. There were a couple of times I'd been late, but Graeme had covered for
20   me. He seems to be quite a good guy and isn't going to say anything to Jennifer. I'm not sure if he knows about my work in Soweto, but I don't think he'd say anything if he did. I've been over there six times now; twice a week. In my first session I had eight boys, ranging in age from seven to

seventeen. There are now around 50 boys who come along. I don't know if we can cope with any more, but I'm not sure how to stop them coming. I love their enthusiasm for the game, and they are so keen to learn everything I am able to teach them.

Amahle has been brilliant – arranging a place for me to train the boys and putting the word around that the local boys should join in. I try to train the boys at the same time as she trains the girls so that we can meet up for a coffee afterwards. I have never met a girl before that is so passionate about football.

Just one scary moment. Yesterday I was in the café with Amahle. She had a coffee, and I had some delicious mango juice. While we were drinking, I saw the short guy with the gold chains. He was standing outside the café, directly behind Amahle but staring directly at me. I've no idea what he was trying to do, but it seems he wanted to intimidate me. Is there something wrong with giving young people in Soweto an outlet for their energy and talent? I don't think so.

20 October 2019: St George's School,
Johannesburg, South Africa

Graeme

7–1! I checked the records, and no team from St George's has ever lost that badly before. Was it because this year's under fifteens are particularly bad, or is it because their coach has got other things on his mind?

One of my colleagues saw him in a taxi heading to Orlando, and he's been disappearing twice a week for the last three weeks. I know the Hector Pieterson Museum is interesting, but it can't be *that* interesting. So why is he going there? My suspicion is that he has found a girlfriend. He's a good-looking lad and he's young, so he won't have a problem finding a nice girl.

I have to say I am disappointed with his lack of commitment to St George's. We've paid a lot of money to fly him over from the UK, and it's not as though he's a qualified teacher – he's only just left his own school. He should be grateful to us, commit to working hard and showing St George's to be the excellent school that it is. I haven't said anything to Jennifer yet, but I think we may have to issue him a warning. I still can't believe it; 7–1!

Chapter Eight

23 October 2019: Orlando, Soweto, South Africa

Amahle

I cannot believe how good Tommy is with the boys. He's friendly and relaxed with them, and firm but fair when he needs to be. The boys adore him. He has fired them with confidence, and I think half of them are sure they'll be playing in Europe in a few years.

I heard from Kungawo that Tommy is having some problems at school. Some of the parents have been complaining about him. Apparently the school football team has not been doing very well and that, say the parents, is Tommy's fault. Kungawo was very curious about me and Tommy – I hope he can accept our friendship. I really like Tommy and I wouldn't want my brother to be against it.

My mum was curious about this *umfana wengisi* that my little brothers talk about all the time. (Both of them go to his training sessions.) She wants him to come for a meal so that she can meet him and get to know what all the fuss is about. My mum's English is not great as her schooling was badly affected by apartheid, but she is a smart woman and she'll find out about him just by observing him – though I'm sure she'll be asking me and my brothers and sisters to translate a few questions for her.

I have no problems with Tommy seeing our house and meeting my family. I can tell that he will accept us as we are. I am a little worried about my mum's cooking though. She's a big fan of samp and chicken feet. Something tells me Tommy will find it difficult to tuck into that.

It's strange, when I'm with Tommy, I don't get much attention, but when he's not with me, I have boys coming up to me, asking if I'd like to go for a walk, have a beer and a *kota* or sometimes just simply if I'd like 'a bit of fun'. What part of the word 'no' don't these boys understand?

14 November 2019: Jack and Joe's flat,
Bloemfontein, South Africa

Jack

"Nice haircut, Tommy!"

"Thanks. I got it done in a barbershop in Orlando."

Tommy's head was shaved at the sides, but the hair on top was still quite long. Joe and I sat next to each other in front of the computer, video conferencing with Tommy and Olivia.

Olivia was dressed in a colourful South African dress that she'd picked up in the local market and her hair was now in dreadlocks. She had definitely got into the spirit of South African culture. She regularly sent us clips of bands that she was watching and could say 'let the world unite in peace, love and friendship' in Xhosa, the most common African language in Cape Town. You may have heard it before, the one with clicks made at the back of the throat. Olivia practised for weeks and is now pretty good at it. She says that she's found where she's meant to be, and everyone is really kind. I'm not sure if 'everyone' includes the man who stole her handbag while she was waiting for the cable car up

Table Mountain, but I'm happy for her. She's enjoying her time in Cape Town.

Tommy, over in Joburg, is not doing so well at school. He's been late for class a few times and, as he admits, his heart isn't really in the job. That came as a surprise. Tommy seemed to be very dedicated, and I just can't imagine him oversleeping or not throwing himself into the job. He's a dark horse. When we spent the week together in Joburg, I'd sometimes look over at him and he'd be a million miles away. I'd love to know what's going on in that head of his.

18 November 2019: St George's School,
Johannesburg, South Africa

Tommy

"Tommy, can I have a word?"

It was Graeme. He was concerned about me. He was getting hell from Jennifer who was getting hell from the parents. Apparently there's a social media group for the parents of our pupils, and the number one topic is me. They say that I'm regularly late for class – not really true. I've been late three times, which, in three months, doesn't seem that bad. They say I can't remember all the boys' names and I insult the boys on the football field. I admit I find it hard to remember all their names, but I don't insult the boys. Okay, I did call one boy 'Peester' instead of Pieter, but that's only because I heard another boy called him 'Peester'. I didn't know that it meant something rude in Afrikaans, and I definitely didn't mean to insult the boy as his parents suggested.

"I really want to help you, Tommy. You seem to be a good guy, but there's something going on. There are stories about you having a girlfriend from the townships, and I've no idea if they're true, but if you need someone to talk to, I'm here and I'm ready to listen, in complete confidence."

So I told him. Well, I told him that I was seeing a girl. We had coffee together and became friends. He didn't need to know all the details, and I think he'd be more upset about the football training than about me seeing Amahle.

Graeme did warn me about the levels of HIV in the townships and told me he knew a good doctor who could treat just about any disease if I needed one.

"Are you feeling okay? No problems ... down there?"

I told him I was fine. I also wondered how he knew about 'good doctors who could treat just about any disease'. Perhaps he had had – or was having – an affair with someone.

My conversation with Graeme got me thinking. Was I 'seeing a girl'? I was definitely seeing a lot of Amahle – and she was, unquestionably, a brilliant person, smart, determined, and had a great love for the people she cared about. Did she care about me? Or was I simply a useful person to know, perhaps a way for her, or her girls, to get in contact with a European football club? I was pretty sure that wasn't the case, but as many people told me, South Africa is a complicated place.

I got a message from Olivia. She says she's dying to meet up and doesn't know if she can wait until Christmas – when we are supposed to meet up with our coordinator. She wants to take a couple of days off work and fly up to Joburg for a few days. Apparently she wants to hang out with me. You can imagine how thrilled I am about that.

Chapter Nine

24 November 2019: Orlando,
Soweto, South Africa

Amahle

What a day. It was Tommy's birthday, and while he didn't
want me to buy him a present, he did agree to let me take
him to a restaurant on Vilakazi Street. I gave him a big card,
signed by all the boys he trains and a small one from me.
After the meal we went to our café for a coffee and a mango
juice. He told me his mum sent over a cake, but it had a layer
of mould on it when he opened the box. I then asked him a
question I've been meaning to ask for months.

"What about your dad? Did he send you anything?"

Tommy looked at me, then he looked away. I saw him
take a very deep breath, then he looked back at me.

"My dad's in prison."

I waited. This was clearly not easy for Tommy. I took his
hand and held it. I could feel that it was shaking slightly.

"He … he had a car accident two years ago. He was
coming to see me play football. I asked him to. It was the
semi-final of the local cup. It wasn't far from where we live,
but my dad was driving too quickly, much too quickly. He
was overtaking a woman on a bike when a truck came
around the corner."

I squeezed Tommy's hand.

"The woman on the bike was taken to hospital and was
put into an induced coma. Three years later, she's still in
that coma. My dad was arrested for dangerous driving. He'll

be in prison for five years. The worst thing is, I blame myself. I know I shouldn't, but he was coming to see me play football. I asked him to come. If I hadn't asked him, he'd still be at home instead of in prison."

What can you say when someone tells you something like that? No words can help. So I said nothing and just continued holding his hand.

We didn't speak until we were standing at the taxi rank. Tommy always waited for me to get my taxi before he jumped in his.

"Thanks for listening. I've never told anyone before."

"That's what friends are for," I said.

Tommy looked at me. We were standing close to each other. Then he leant in and our lips touched, very gently, then as he moved in for a second time, I moved back slightly.

"Is something wrong?" he asked. "I thought we ... I mean ... I thought you ..."

"Nothing's wrong at all, Tommy. I like you a lot. I think you're fantastic. You're an amazing guy."

"But? You've already got a boyfriend?"

"No, Tommy; I've already got a girlfriend."

26 November 2019: St George's School,
Johannesburg, South Africa

Kungawo

Of course, I knew about Tommy and his football training in Orlando. My two little brothers train with him and they're really happy with what he does. They say he's passionate, knowledgeable, kind and funny. That's interesting because at St George's he may be knowledgeable about football, but he's definitely not passionate, kind or funny while he's here. It's like he's a robot, just going through the motions. He's friendly towards me, but with the other staff and the pupils he is cool, some would say 'unfriendly'. He definitely doesn't go the extra mile as the good teachers do. Or perhaps 'going the extra mile' in Tommy's case is jumping in a taxi and heading off to Orlando.

But what did surprise me was the news I got from a friend of mine. There had been talk of Tommy having a girlfriend in Soweto, but I was quite surprised to find out who it was. My friend told me that he saw my sister in a café with a white guy with blond hair. Apparently they were holding hands. Now I have no problem with Tommy and my sister getting together, but it was a surprise because some people in Orlando say that my sister prefers girls to boys. At first I thought that some guy had asked her out, and when she said no, he told her she must be a lesbian.

It was about six months ago my little brother, Bandile, who is nine, couldn't stop laughing when I saw him. He told me he was with his brother Desmond when they saw Amahle and another girl kissing.

"Do you mean kissing when they say 'hello' or 'goodbye'?"

"No, I mean they were kissing!" He kissed the air around him trying to show me how Amahle and her friend had been kissing.

So if Amahle is now with Tommy, that means that Bandile was wrong. Amahle will still have problems from some people who will think that she has found a sugar daddy, but I'm sure my sister wouldn't want a sugar daddy. If she's with

Tommy, it's because she loves him – and I sincerely hope he loves her.

Tommy

I feel so much better now that I've told someone about my dad. 'A problem shared is a problem halved' is something my granny used to say. Now I realise how true it is. I will always feel guilty about what happened to my dad, but it is no longer my big secret – at least not with Amahle.

Ah, Amahle. I'm happy to say that what happened between us last week hasn't affected our friendship at all. I have no problem with Amahle being in a relationship with a girl – and she's happy that we can still be friends. If anything, our friendship is growing stronger now that everything is out in the open.

A couple of days ago I was in a café with Amahle drinking coffee and mango juice. We were talking about football and about the possibility of arranging some games for my boys. While we were chatting, I saw some guys in the corner of the café. One of them took out a small bag and poured out some stones which were small and shiny.

"Amahle," I whispered. "There are two guys behind you, and I think they're dealing in diamonds."

Amahle looked around casually, then laughed. "Those guys," she whispered, "are dealing in shiny stones. It's a common trick here in Soweto. Someone tells a tourist that they work in a diamond mine and have some rough diamonds to sell. The tourist gets to buy some shiny stones for a few hundred dollars."

"So no real diamonds then."

"Sadly not," said Amahle. "If they were real diamonds, I don't think those guys would be living in Orlando."

I was just about to finish my mango juice when a rough-looking guy came in and bought a bottle of beer. He stood at the bar but stared shamelessly at Amahle.

Amahle spoke to me in that quiet, slightly husky voice of hers. "Tommy, can you do me a favour?"

I had no idea what kind of favour Amahle wanted. I knew she was not rich, but she had never asked me for anything before.

"Sure, what can I do for you?"

"Could you put down your mango juice and kiss me like I'm your girlfriend?"

I understood what she wanted. *"Ayikho inkinga."*

I leant over and embraced her as our lips met.

I haven't kissed many girls in my life, but kissing Amahle was the best kiss I've ever had. Out of the corner of my eye I saw the guy at the bar walk out of the café, leaving most of his beer behind.

"Ngiyabona," said Amahle.

"*Sho.* Any time," I said – and we both laughed.

Amahle explained the difficult position gay women found themselves in. Some men just couldn't accept that she preferred being with Kaya, her girlfriend, rather than a man. She told me there are some guys who feel gay women need 'correcting'. I'm pretty sure I understand what she meant, and it makes me sick just thinking about it.

On a brighter note, Amahle's mother has invited me for dinner on Friday. I'm quite looking forward to some home-cooked food. It will be just me, Amahle, her mum and her two little sisters. I'm looking forward to meeting them all.

Chapter Ten

3 December 2019: Waterbridge
School, Bristol, England

Ms Manifold

You can't help worrying about your pupils – particularly the ones you really care about. As it was my idea that Tommy should go to South Africa, I feel even more responsible. He sends me an email now and again and tells me what's
5 going on. My replies to him must sound very boring: I fell off my bike last week. I caught two girls smoking behind the sixth form block. I got a new microscope for the biology department.

Meanwhile he is in Soweto kissing a gay girl to frighten
10 off some weird guy in a bar, training a bunch of 50 children and paying for the balls and nets out of his own pocket.

I remember the job he was sent to do was at a school called St George's, but he doesn't seem to mention that very often. I presume he's still working there, but it is clear where
15 his passion and energy is.

He told me he's going to have dinner with Amahle's family. What a great education for him seeing how different people live around the world. I really hope it all works out for him.

Amahle

"Eat, Tommy, eat. It's good, no?"

"It's very good. *Ngiyabona*," said Tommy. "But I'm full now."

Tommy rubbed his stomach to show my mother that she
5 had fed him well. I was impressed that he had managed to
eat a big bowl of samp and even managed to get something
from the pile of chicken feet that my mother had prepared.

Our house is a very simple one with a shared toilet, and
we get our water from the standpipe down the road. The
10 metal roof means that when it rains, you can't hear yourself
think, and in summer, like now, it makes the house pretty
warm. But Tommy didn't seem to mind at all. He stretched
out on the sofa and smiled at mum. Her English is not great,
so I had translated her questions and Tommy's answers:
15 No, Tommy didn't know Queen Elizabeth personally, but he
had seen Buckingham Palace. Yes, he knew Nelson Mandela,
Desmond Tutu and Steve Biko. Yes, he was optimistic about
the future of South Africa and yes, he thought that one day
I would make someone very happy.

20 I could tell my mum liked him. She had that dreamy look
on her face like when she's watching a romantic film. She
asked me to come and help her with the washing up so that
she could tell me what she thought of him. Of course, that
wasn't necessary as Tommy's Zulu is limited to a few words
25 and phrases – which I have to say, he impressed my mum
with. So while my mum told me what she thought of the
umfana wengisi, Tommy was left to entertain, or be enter-

tained by Enzokuhle and Omphile, my two sisters. I think he'd seen them in one of my training sessions, so I hoped they would talk about football.

After Tommy had gone home, they explained that Tommy had asked for some phrases in Zulu. Something he could shout at the boys when they are training, and he wants them to work harder. My sisters are 13 and 15, and I think they're great football players. Perhaps they could be teachers one day – after their footballing careers of course.

5 December 2019: St George's School,
Johannesburg, South Africa

Tommy

"So how did you like the chicken feet?"

"It was ... not as bad as I thought," I said, smiling.

Kungawo was waiting to take a group of boys to the swimming baths. I was waiting for the under-fifteen squad to get changed, so we could get in a couple of hours of practice. I wanted to work on their defence. They seem to have no awareness about how to defend the goal and to protect the keeper. They just seem to run at the ball and boot it upfield if they get the chance.

"My mum likes you," said Kungawo. "She's very happy about your ... friendship with Amahle."

I noticed that Kungawo paused before the word 'friendship'. I think he was trying to find out more about my ... friendship with his sister. I like Kungawo. I think he's a good guy who works hard, but I don't feel I need to talk about whatever is going on, or rather not going on, between me and Amahle.

"That's good to hear. Your mum is a good woman. It can't be easy bringing up five children in Soweto."

5 "Very true. Since my dad was killed, she has devoted herself to looking after us, and luckily I can support her with whatever I get from the school."

I couldn't believe how stupid I'd been. I told Amahle about my dad being in prison and not thought to ask 10 about hers. I couldn't have known he was dead, but I should have asked.

"I'm sorry, I didn't know about your dad."

Kungawo explained what happened. His father had been in a bar in Orlando, having a quiet drink with his 15 brother, Kungawo's uncle, Bokamoso. Suddenly there were shots outside. His uncle dived under the table, but Kungawo's dad was too slow. A bullet hit him in the chest. He died three days later.

"Apparently it was a disagreement between two drug 20 gangs, and there was a drive-by shooting to scare off a rival gang. One gang drove up to the bar and fired at some gang members standing outside. The bullets missed the gang members, but hit my dad who was having a quiet drink inside."

25 "I'm really sorry to hear that. Did the police catch them?"

Kungawo shook his head. "The police have enough problems without trying to sort out fights between drug gangs. We have our suspicions, but there's not a lot we can do about it."

Chapter Eleven

6 December 2019: Tommy's home,
Bristol, England

Wendy

I'm so glad that Tommy is doing well in South Africa. To be honest, I was really nervous about him going, but nothing can stop my Tommy when he gets an idea in his head. He sends me an email with lots of photos once a week, and we
5 have a video chat once every two weeks. I'm really impressed with how he can do his job at St George's *and* help out the boys in the townships. At first, I thought he was really brave going to Soweto, but from the photos he's sent me it doesn't look that bad at all.

10 Between you and me, I think he might be in love. He keeps mentioning a girl called Amahle: 'Amahle is amazing as she works as a teaching assistant in the morning, then does football training in the afternoon. She even helps her sisters and brothers with their homework in the evening.
15 Amahle was brilliant in organising somewhere for me to train a group of boys. Amahle has shown me a very different world ...'

I'm very happy that he seems to be happy for the first time in years. I know it hasn't been easy for Tommy with his
20 dad not being around, but perhaps the change of environment was exactly what he needed. It does sound like a very different world. A couple of nights ago he had chicken feet for dinner! Weird or what?

Jennifer

"I can't tell you everything he said, but he's definitely seeing a girl in the townships. He says he wants to carry on working here, but he also wants to carry on seeing his girlfriend."

"Thank you, Graeme. So Tommy Gilmour wants free accommodation and free food at St George's, but he doesn't really want to be a part of the school. He just wants to spend all his time with his …"

Graeme interrupted me. "To be fair, we can't tell him what to do in his free time."

"To be fair to the parents and pupils of St George's, should we really keep him employed here? We could send him back to the UK – that would be one way of stopping him seeing his … special friend."

I just don't get it. South Africa is a developing country. St George's is doing its best to support that development by giving the young people of South Africa the best education possible, white and black. They are the future of this country, and I want every teacher in this school to dedicate themselves 100% to their work and with HIJ: honesty, integrity and justice. What kind of message does it send out to our pupils if one of the teachers is dishonest and lacks integrity and is not fully committed? Why should they give 100% when he is only giving 50%?

We've had many people from England working in this school, and most of them are idealists that think that by spending a year in a school in South Africa they can make a change. And they *do* make a change. They move their little grain of sand in the very big desert of injustice. I couldn't ask for more. St George's is now a multi-racial school with the percentage of non-white students up to 12% and we offer five scholarships a year to black South Africans. We're doing our bit and we expect our teachers to do their bit as well – and 99% of them are. There's just a certain Tommy Gilmour who is not pulling his weight. It really is time to do something – for the sake of St George's. I called Tommy on that nasty little mobile of his. "Tommy, can you come to my office?"

"Well, actually I ..."

"Now, Tommy!"

"*Sharp*, I'll come over."

As he came into my office I stood up and held up a yellow card.

"This is your warning, Tommy Gilmour. Any more lateness to class, any more being offensive to the pupils of this school, any more poor behaviour at all – and I will have no hesitation in showing you the red card. That means that you will go back to England on the earliest flight available. Got that?"

"I get it," he said.

Did he really get it? Did he really care? I have no idea what's going on in that boy's head.

Tommy

"That's okay, Tommy. It's in the past now," said Amahle as we hugged.

I can't believe how calm she was. Her dad was shot dead, and she is so calm about it. I wanted to tell her how sorry I was, how ashamed I was that I had told her all about my dad without asking about hers.

"Of course, I miss him, we all do. He was a fantastic father to us all, but life goes on."

We were in our regular café, drinking our usual drinks. I needed someone to talk to about what was happening at St George's, but I couldn't forget how thoughtless I had been to Amahle and her dad.

"So, let's move on. How are things at school? I hear from Kungawo that there's a new referee in town."

From the smile on her face, Amahle knew about my yellow card from Jennifer. Did she really think it was funny? Jennifer said she would send me back to England if I stepped out of line again.

"Don't worry about it," said Amahle, reading my mind. "She can't get rid of you. How is she going to find a replacement at such short notice? I really can't believe that you won't be here for your whole year. I think she is more likely to leave than you are."

Is that what she wanted to believe, or did she genuinely believe it?

"Kungawo tells me she's under a lot of stress at the moment though he isn't entirely sure why."

Chapter Twelve

*11 December 2019: St George's School,
Johannesburg, South Africa*

Olivia

"Olive, I didn't expect to see you here."

"It's Olivia, actually," I replied.

"Olivia, of course, yes, I'm sorry. Australia, Epsom, Cape Town, right?"

5 "That's right. You've got a good memory."

"Thank you. I do try my best."

I thought I would drop in and see the coordinator of our project while I was here. Let her know how brilliant things are down in Cape Town. I remembered where her 10 office was from our first week in Joburg when we first arrived. That seems like a hundred years ago now – it is incredible that it is barely three months ago.

I was about to knock on her door when the door opened. Jennifer was talking Afrikaans with a tall man with a military 15 style haircut.

I saw a sudden look of panic on Jennifer's face, but that was quickly replaced by her usual beaming smile as she waved goodbye to her previous visitor and welcomed me into her office.

20 "So how is Victoria?" asked Jennifer, referring to the head teacher of the school I work in.

"She's, like, really cool. All the girls love her. She's a great woman to work for. In fact, she …"

"Sorry, Olivia, could I just ask you to open the window? It's a little warm in here."

"Um, sure," I said. I stood up, opened the window slightly and sat back down.

5 "So, tell me all about Victoria, Cape Town, and your amazing hair!" said a far more relaxed Jennifer.

As I told her about the music clubs that I went to and all the friends I had made, I couldn't help noticing that something had changed. Before I opened the window there 10 was a thick blue envelope at the side of Jennifer's desk, not very well hidden by Jennifer's handbag. It was no longer there, probably now safely inside Jennifer's desk. The envelope was not particularly big, maybe 15cm by 6cm. What was inside? I had a good idea. Why didn't Jennifer want me 15 to see it? I guess it was none of my business.

11 December 2019: a music club,
Johannesburg, South Africa

Tommy

"Oh come on, Tommy, this club is, like, really boring. Take me to another one!"

"Aren't you tired, Olivia? You've had a long day."

"I'll sleep when I'm in my grave. Come on, Tommy! It's 20 Friday night. Let's party!"

"Ayikho inkinga."

So we left the club where two black guys were playing Bob Marley songs to a largely white audience and went in search of some 'like, really authentic African sounds'.

"This looks like a cool place," said Olivia and pulled me into a small bar which was playing music far too loud for my taste.

"This place is, like, amazing! I can't believe you haven't been here before."

I confess that I'm not a big fan of music. Many of the other students back in Bristol were into EDM, I preferred kicking a ball about with a few friends. Also, my grandad was pretty deaf in his fifties and sixties, and I don't think he went to many EDM parties in his youth. I'm trying to look after my ears.

I watched as Olivia wormed her way to the bar. I can't be sure, but I think I recognised the guy who, it seemed, was trying to pick her up. But it clearly wasn't his lucky night as seconds later, Olivia returned with two cans.

"Don't you just love Zamalek?" she said, handing me a can.

I confessed I didn't know what it was.

"You know, black label, South African beer. They call it Zamalek – not sure why. Cheers!"

Olivia took a long gulp of her beer. I sipped on mine. I rarely drink beer. I'm not particularly fond of the taste, and I don't want to repeat the one night when I got drunk and spent the next morning puking up four pints of lager and a kebab.

"Come on, let's dance!"

"I'm good, thanks, Olivia. I'll stay here and look after your beer."

I could see she was tempted to grab my arm and drag me onto the dance floor but decided against it. "*Sharp,* see you later!"

I watched as Olivia danced a few metres in front of the band, her long blonde dreadlocks flying around her head. In some ways it would be nice to be like Olivia. She is definitely a free spirit and is really positive about life. It's just not the way I am. I am passionate about things I believe in, but it always seems to stay inside me. I don't show my emotions, even when I told Amahle about my dad, there were no tears. Perhaps Olivia has got it right. Let your emotions out rather than keeping them bottled up inside.

Olivia was getting plenty of attention on the dance floor. Plenty of guys danced close to her. I watched as they tried to chat to Olivia, and she would exchange a friendly word but then went back to her dancing. Occasionally she would wave at me or encourage me to join her on the dance floor. I smiled and sipped at my Zamalek.

After about five songs, Olivia returned and took a long drink of her beer. "Ah, I needed that."

"The dance or the beer?"

"Both!" laughed Olivia. "Come on, let's go for a walk!"

She grabbed my hand and led me out of the bar. I could still feel the ringing in my ears, but I was more concerned about my hand; Olivia was still holding it as we walked along. As we passed a bench she jumped up on the bench so that she was taller than me. She then reached forward and held my head as she moved in for a kiss.

Amahle

"So you're the lucky girl," said Olivia as she shook my hand.

"Lucky girl?" I wasn't quite sure what she meant.

"Tommy's girlfriend. He told me, like, *all* about you last night."

5   I smiled. "Nothing bad I hope."

"Not at all. I wanted to kiss him last night, but he stopped me and told me about his special girlfriend. He's like, Amahle is so amazing, and Amahle works so hard, and Amahle looks after her little sisters and brothers AND
10 works as a teaching assistant AND runs training sessions for teenage girls. I'm like wow!"

"That's my Tommy," I said, smiling, and patting him on the leg. Tommy smiled back at me. Olivia smiled at both of us.

15 Despite all the smiles, it was clear to me that Olivia knew that we weren't really a couple, and it was pretty clear to me that she liked Tommy – but, for whatever reason, Tommy did not feel the same way.

We talked about England and Australia for a while but
20 then quickly got onto our favourite subject, football. I'm not sure how keen Olivia was, but she is a passionate girl who loves to talk.

"So if you're training all these boys, do they actually play games or do they just kick a ball around?" Olivia asked
25 Tommy.

I could see that the phrase 'just kick a ball around' hurt him. I know that he is a dedicated football player and has taught the boys, including my brothers, a lot about football, not just the physical skills, but also the mental strength they need to succeed on the pitch.

"Well, we play little five-a-side games, but I guess you're
5 right, I should organise a proper game." Then he looked at me. "Amahle? Can you help me fix it?"

"*Ayikho inkinga.* In fact, I know a teacher at a school called St George's. I might ask him if he can put up a team," I said.

Tommy smiled. "I wish it were possible, Amahle, but I
10 don't think that's a great idea at the moment."

No problem. There are plenty of teams in Soweto who would welcome the chance to play a match. I'm sure I can find a team for Tommy to play against.

Chapter Thirteen

13 December 2019: Cape Town, South Africa

Olivia

"She's not your girlfriend, is she?"

"Well, not exactly."

"Tommy, please don't treat me like I'm stupid."

"Okay, okay, she's not my girlfriend – but we are very good
friends."

Just because I have blonde hair and say 'like' too much,
doesn't mean that I'm stupid. Yes, I know everyone makes
fun of me for using 'like' a lot, but that's how all my schoolfriends spoke, and I just picked up the same way of talking.
There's always a desire to fit in, and speaking like your
schoolmates is one way of doing it. It's not easy fitting
in when you move to a different place. I know everybody
thinks I am a happy, smiling airhead, but they don't know
the real me: the Olivia who cries herself to sleep at night.
The Olivia whose hands are shaking as she delivers her
lessons. The Olivia who is sometimes sick with worry before
an important meeting.

Yes, I am angry. I'm not angry with Tommy for not
wanting to kiss me, but I am angry with him for lying to me.
Why do people do that? I was looking forward to spending
a weekend with someone I like and admire – but I ended up
coming home a day early. It cost me a bit to change my ticket
at such short notice, but it was worth it. Tommy did try to
apologise, but I just felt like shit and wanted to be on my
own. Everybody has days like this, don't they?

13 December 2019: St George's School,
Johannesburg, South Africa

Tommy

I really don't know how to behave when someone gets
angry with me – particularly when that anger is justified. I
shouldn't have lied to Olivia. I should have treated her
like the eighteen-year-old she is – not like she's eight.

5 I have to say she handled it very well. She was pretty calm
with Amahle – and even in our conversation on the way back
to the guesthouse where she stayed, I could sense her anger,
but we talked about Jack and Joe in Bloemfontein, about
South African music and perhaps most interestingly about
10 our coordinator, and my boss, Jennifer Goodfellow.

Olivia is better at keeping in touch with Jack and Joe.
They're both doing fine, a little homesick, but they have each
other. They're looking forward to meeting up at Christmas.

She's pretty passionate about her music and has bought
15 herself a djembe drum. She's taking lessons in a place on
Long Street in Cape Town. I can well imagine she'll be in a
band before her year is up.

I was talking to her about money. I think we get the same
amount of money from our schools – which I am sure is *a*
20 *lot* less than the other teachers get as we are 'only' students
and we get a free place to stay and free flights from the UK.
I mentioned I was a bit short of money as it was not easy
for me to get to a bank because I'm either teaching at school
or I'm over in Orlando training the boys.

25 Olivia suggested I get Jennifer to pay me in cash, but I
explained that that wasn't possible as our school has a strict

'no cash' policy to avoid corruption. The parents pay via bank transfer, and we are paid via bank transfer.

"So perhaps I didn't see an envelope full of banknotes on Jennifer's desk then."

5   "What?"

"I can't be certain, but Jennifer was acting very strangely. She asked me to open the window as she was warm – although her air conditioning was on. When I turned back to her, the thick envelope wasn't there."

10   We couldn't prove that Jennifer was doing anything wrong, but I definitely had my suspicions. What was it she told us? HIJ: honesty, integrity and justice. Did Jennifer stick to HIJ, or was it one rule for us and another rule for them? If she is guilty of accepting bundles of cash and she finds out

15   that I know about it, she'll put me on the next plane back to England. Whatever I do, I'll have to do it very carefully.

17 December 2019: Meadowlands,
Soweto, South Africa

Bandile Nyembezi (Amahle's youngest brother)

What a day! My wonderful sister Amahle organised a match for us. Our team is the Orlando Under Twelves. We played against Meadowlands Under Thirteens – and guess what?

20   We won! My brother Desmond scored two goals and I nearly scored one as well.

Coach Tommy organised a taxi for us to travel over to Meadowlands. We went past the amazing stadium that was used in the 2010 World Cup. I don't remember that because I was only just born.

The Meadowlands boys were bigger than us and they had some nice kit as well. Their football pitch was a real one. It was *so* big – and it was flat! Where we train, the ground is full of holes, and there's not a lot of grass.

I have to tell you what happened in the second half of the game. We were losing 2–0. Coach Tommy was shouting instructions to us, and we were putting Meadowlands under a lot of pressure.

The ball went out for a throw in, and I stopped to tie up my boots. I was not too far from Coach Tommy. I saw him look at a piece of paper in his pocket, then he called out to me. "Bandile! Bandile!"

I looked over to where he was standing.

"Bandile! *Ngiyingane enkulu!*"

I couldn't believe my ears. Did Coach Tommy really just say *'Ngiyingane enkulu!'*?

"Ngiyingane enkulu!" he shouted again, waving me forward towards the Meadowlands penalty area.

I ran forward but looked back at Tommy. A few metres away from him, the Meadowlands coach was doubled up with laughter.

When I looked back, two players crashed together, and the ball bounced back to me.

"Cross it, Bandile!" shouted Desmond who was waiting in the box.

In training, Coach Tommy makes us practise shots with a lot of curl on them. I saw the goalkeeper was off his line, so I kicked the ball towards Desmond. The ball curled in the air and … hit the crossbar. It bounced back out, and Desmond was there to kick it in. 2–1.

Coach Tommy gave me the thumbs up as I ran back into position. I was sure we could win it now.

Minutes later, one of our players was pulled down in the penalty area, and we were awarded a penalty. My friend Solomon is our penalty taker and he had no problems scoring our second goal.

With about five minutes to go, we were pushing for the winning goal. We had a free kick between the halfway line and the penalty area. My brother Desmond ran over to take it.

"Desmond!" I think everyone on the pitch could hear Coach Tommy.

"Ngidinga ukunya!"

Even the Meadowlands players were laughing. Coach Tommy tried again. *"Ngidinga ukunya ngokushesha!"*

Even the referee had a big smile on his face this time. Coach Tommy had no idea what the problem was. Finally my brother calmed down enough to take the free kick. The ball curled beautifully through the air – and went into the top corner!

Minutes later the referee blew his whistle. I don't think I have ever been so happy. 3–2, against Meadowlands!

In the taxi on the way home we sang songs together. When a song finished someone shouted, *"Ngiyingane enkulu!"* And we all repeated it. Someone else shouted, *"Ngidinga ukunya!"* And we all replied, *"Ngokushesha!"*

I don't know where Coach Tommy learnt his Zulu, but I think he should ask for his money back.

Chapter Fourteen

*17 December 2019: Orlando,
Soweto, South Africa*

Tommy

"Say it again!"

"*Ngiyingane enkulu!*" I said.

I don't think I have ever heard Amahle laugh so loud.

"You actually shouted that to Bandile on the football
pitch?"

"Yes, I thought it meant 'Go forward and attack'."

Amahle laughed again.

"So come on, Amahle. What does '*Ngiyingane enkulu!*'
mean?"

"It means, ..." she had problems speaking as she was
laughing so much. "It means, 'I am a big baby'."

As Amahle collapsed with laughter again, I thought back
to that evening in Amahle's house, sitting with Enzokuhle
and Omphile, asking them for simple phrases in Zulu that I
could shout to the players. They looked so serious as they
told me 'translations' of the phrases I asked for.

"And the other phrase? I wanted to say something like,
'Do your best – for the team'."

"And what *did* you say?"

"*Ngidinga ukunya ngokushesha!*"

I thought Amahle was going to injure herself, she was
laughing so loud. She then retold the story for the others in
the café – and they joined in her helpless laughter.

"So come on, Amahle, you have to tell me what it means."

She couldn't; she was laughing too much. It was the waitress who finally told me.

"*'Ngidinga ukunya'* means 'I need a shit'."

"Oh no! And what about *'Ngidinga ukunya ngokushesha'?*"

5 "It means 'I need a shit – urgently'."

I looked back at the scene at Meadowlands: five minutes to go, I want to shout encouragement to Amahle's brother Desmond, 'Do your best – for the team.' Instead I shouted, 'I need a shit – urgently!'

10 Well played, Enzokuhle and Omphile. Well played. You definitely got me there.

23 December 2019: Kruger National Park, South Africa

Jack

"Did you get it?"

"I think so," said Joe. "We can check it tonight."

I was sure Joe had got it all. He's brilliant with his camera.
15 We had seen the lionesses waiting silently in the grass, their bodies ready for the kill. A few metres away were some gazelles, munching happily on the grass, apparently unaware of the predators a few metres away. Suddenly the gazelles started running with the lionesses setting off a
20 millisecond later. The gazelles were literally running for their lives, zigzagging across the plain, their only real chance being that the lionesses would tire quickly. But on this occasion the lionesses would not go hungry. One lioness got its front paws – and claws – onto the back of the slowest
25 gazelle, bringing it quickly down into the dust.

So how did we get to the Kruger National Park? Well, our journey started on the 20th of December when Joe and I took the bus for six and a half hours from Bloemfontein to Johannesburg. I slept for most of the journey; Joe filmed anything he could see out of the window. I think he wants to work in the film industry one day.

We spent the evening with Tommy who filled us in on many of the things that were going on his life. I got the impression he wasn't telling us the whole story. This girl Amahle seems to play a pretty important part in his life, and I don't think their only common interest is football.

On the 21st, Olivia came up from Cape Town. It was good to see her again – she's definitely changed from when we first met her in August. In particular, she behaves very strangely when she's around Tommy. Is there something going on between Tommy and Olivia?

On the evening of the 21st, Jennifer Goodfellow, our boss, took us out for a meal. She was friendly and keen to know how we were getting on in our different projects, but I have to say she seemed distracted. It's clear she's not happy with Tommy, but there is definitely something else that is troubling her. Towards the end of our meal, she left us to go and talk to a couple of old school friends at another table. Joe was happily filming as much South African food as he could. He's planning a YouTube channel all about South Africa.

At the end of the evening Jennifer thought we might want to go out partying, but the four of us decided we wanted an early night. Is this normal behaviour for eighteen-year-olds?

On the morning of the 22nd, at 5.30, Kungawo picked us up from the guest house where we were staying. Tommy was already sitting in the minibus. Joe and I joined him in the back, Olivia jumped in next to Kungawo. We then had a ten-hour drive eastwards from Johannesburg to the Kruger National Park. This time I stayed awake and was amazed at what a beautiful country South Africa is with a stunning range of landscapes unlike anything you can see in Europe. We arrived in the early evening and stayed in a guest house near the national park. It is a slightly weird experience trying to get to sleep but being kept awake by roaring lions.

On the 23rd, we got up early, and after a quick breakfast of pap and eggs, we set off into the park. I've been to safari parks in Britain, but nothing compares to seeing animals in their natural habitat. I *loved* the get-out points, places where we could safely get out of the minibus and observe the animals. My favourite time was when we were at a watering hole, watching some lions drinking on one side and some nervous-looking impalas drinking on the other. Olivia snapped away with her fancy camera; Joe videoed everything he could see. Tommy and I just sat and watched. As you can imagine, it was stunning.

It was early evening when Kungawo spotted the pride of lionesses in the grass. He indicated that we should be silent and watch.

We waited for about 20 minutes in absolute silence, Joe's finger poised on the record button of his camera.

It is easy to study natural selection at school, but seeing it in action on the ground in Africa brings it to life – or in the case of the gazelle – to death.

Chapter Fifteen

29 December 2019: Cape Town,
South Africa

Olivia

Christmas 2019 was a pretty weird one for me. First there was Jennifer's meal when she seemed to go out of her way to praise me, Joe and Jack for our hard work, dedication, understanding and empathy. That just made it obvious that she felt Tommy was like the opposite to us.

The Kruger National Park was pretty cool though I prefer some of the smaller national parks near Cape Town. Yes, we saw four of the Big Five, but I don't think like that. I don't see the natural world as names that can be crossed off a list. I care about them and have decided that in the New Year I'm going to stop eating meat completely.

But enough about animals. I got to know Joe and Jack over the Christmas break. Joe is nuts about his filming and showed us some amazing short films he's made about his time in South Africa. Jack is quiet but a very kind guy. Nothing seems to trouble him, so he is a good guy to have around when things go wrong – as they often do in South Africa.

And then there's the enigma, Tommy Gilmour. I am pretty mixed up about my feelings for Tommy. I can see that he's got a good heart, but I find it hard to forgive him for lying to me.

But there was something pretty surprising that happened at the Kruger National Park. We were sitting at the

guest house on our last evening when Joe said he had something to show us. He put his laptop on the table and showed us a short clip, not from the national park but from Jennifer's party. There was a brief shot of Jennifer talking to
5   her old school friends.

"I was curious to find out who she was chatting to," said Joe.

"How can you do that?" I asked. "They weren't wearing name tags."

10   "I took a clear image of the two men from my video. I then did a reverse image search to see if I could find a match with either of the two faces."

"And?" asked Tommy, now interested in what Joe was saying.

15   "Well, I couldn't get a match with the guy with brown hair, but this guy, with the bald head, turns out to be an interesting character. His name is Patrick Vorster. He is involved in local politics, but he's also been in prison for illegally selling uncut diamonds."

20   "I know the name 'Vorster'," said Tommy. "I think there are four of them at my school."

"Correct," said Joe. Patrick Vorster has five children. His four boys go to your school. Another interesting point, Patrick Vorster is ten years younger than Jennifer, so it's
25   unlikely they were at school together."

Something was playing on my mind. "Joe, could you play that clip with Jennifer and Patrick again?"

Joe played the seven-second clip. Yes, there it was. Not easy to see, but I recognised the envelope. The same fat blue
30   envelope I'd seen on Jennifer's desk.

Tommy

"Happy New Year, Tommy."

"Let's hope 2020 will bring you success and happiness."

"Ngiyabona."

We embraced. After the Christmas break it was good to
be back with Amahle again. She told me all about her
Christmas with all her family, well, all except Kungawo
who was with us in the Kruger National Park. It was good to
hear about normal things: presents, singing Christmas
songs, eating a special South African Christmas dinner.

What a contrast with what was happening elsewhere.
That was great work from Joe to find out about Patrick
Vorster, and I'm impressed that Olivia noticed the same
envelope that she'd seen in Jennifer's office. The difficult
part was putting it all together – like the pieces of a jigsaw
puzzle. It seemed that Jennifer was accepting cash from
some of the parents and then perhaps using the money to
buy uncut diamonds. But why?

Amahle

It was good to see Tommy again. I love my family and I had
a great Christmas with them. I love Kaya, my girlfriend; we
had a lovely quiet dinner at New Year. But Tommy is also an
important part of my life. Now that he knows about Kaya, I

feel I can talk about anything with him. Of course, we talk a lot about football. Tommy asked me why I don't play in a team myself.

"When I was six months old, I nearly died. The doctors found that I had a problem with my heart, and I had an operation which saved my life. Throughout my childhood I had regular tests and I seemed to be doing okay. But the doctors warned me not to overdo it. Sadly that rules out a career as a football player. I play occasionally for the Orlando Ladies team but not that often."

"But it doesn't stop you being the world's best football coach," said Tommy. "I really hope you're picked up by one of the big clubs as a coach. You do amazing work with your girls."

"And you don't do too badly with your boys," I replied. "After your victory against Meadowlands, I've got another opponent lined up for you."

"Who is it?"

"I can't tell you yet," I said. "It's a work in progress."

We don't only talk about football. We talk about South Africa and its future. We talk about being gay in different parts of the world. He tells me that he had a couple of gay friends at school, and everybody knew they were gay, and nobody gave them any trouble. How I wish that were true in South Africa. It is so sad that I have to keep Kaya a secret from almost everyone. I can't even tell my own mother. She regularly asks me when Tommy and I are going to get married.

After our long chat in the café, Tommy and I walked slowly down to the taxi stop.

"So when am I going to see you again?"

"That's a good question," said Tommy. "Let me consult my diary."

Tommy pulled out his phone and tapped in his pin code. "Let me see …"

Suddenly there was a loud noise across the street. Some men were arguing, pushing and shoving each other. Immediately I held my bag close to me. This was a classic distraction technique. Unfortunately Tommy didn't know about it and continued looking at his phone.

"Tommy!" I cried.

A young boy ran close to Tommy, snatched his phone, and ran into the street. An older boy appeared on a motorbike, the young boy jumped on the back and they disappeared into the night.

"Shit happens," said Tommy. "It's no big deal. It was pretty old anyway."

"I don't think they wanted your phone, Tommy," I said. "They want to see the messages on it; all the messages we've exchanged. They want the clear evidence they need that I'm gay – and now they've got it."

Chapter Sixteen

9 January 2020: St George's School,
Johannesburg, South Africa

Kungawo

"And you won't tell me what's wrong?"

"I can't," said Amahle. "Maybe it's nothing to worry about at all."

I have never seen my sister like this before. Strong, confident Amahle, who has no problem dealing with all sorts of
difficult situations, seems to have lost her spark. My mind
is racing to try to work out what it can be. I went to see my
family as soon as I got back from Kruger and everything
seemed fine. I spent a lovely day with my mum and my
brothers and sisters. I took them out for an ice cream, and
we had a lovely time together. So what has happened since
then? Something pretty serious.

While I was on the trip to Kruger, I slept in the same guest
house as Tommy and the others. One evening I had an early
night, but it was a warm night, and I couldn't sleep. The
rooms didn't have windows, just metal screens to keep out
the mosquitos. Tommy and Olivia were chatting about
lots of things, and now I understand why things had been
frosty between Olivia and Tommy. I'd had my suspicions
about my sister being gay, but now I knew it for sure. But
she was gay before Christmas, why should she be behaving
so strangely after Christmas? Has she split up from her
girlfriend? Or is something else troubling her?

I also heard Tommy and Olivia talking about Jennifer. It was no great surprise to me that she is involved in some kind of dodgy business.

"But why would she buy uncut diamonds when she already has the cash?" asked Tommy.

"We don't *know* that she's buying diamonds," said Olivia. "We just know that she gave Patrick Vorster a thick envelope which was probably full of money. We didn't see him give her anything."

"True, but we didn't watch them all evening. We were pretty lucky to have Joe's video of Jennifer, Patrick and the envelope."

If it's true about the diamonds, and I can believe it is, I know why she did it. Diamonds are high value and small – easy for her to take out of the country and sell at a good profit.

But there's no proof. Just because she met with a guy who used to deal in uncut diamonds, and it appears that she gave him some money, does that mean we should call the police and have her arrested? Not at all. Jennifer Goodfellow is a respected member of Johannesburg society. The police aren't going to do anything unless we have real proof. But how could we get it? I have one idea, but it is risky. I've been working at the school for quite a few years, but I'm sure Jennifer would be very happy to get rid of me if she thought I was looking for evidence in her office.

Another thing I'd like to find out more about: why is my sister so upset? I can't help thinking that Tommy is involved somehow. What could he have done to upset her? They *seemed* to have a good friendship – have they had a row about something? If so, what? Life is complicated sometimes. I'm not sure what steps I'll take, but whatever I do, those steps will have to be careful.

Chapter Seventeen

15 January 2020: St George's School,
Johannesburg, South Africa

Jennifer

"I want to apologise, Jennifer," said Tommy. "I realise I haven't made a good start at St George's, but this year will be different. I guarantee you'll see big changes."

Do you know the expression 'a leopard can't change its
5   spots'? The same is very true of a little liar like Tommy Gilmour. He's devious, lazy and not even a good liar – and I now know where he gets it from. I called his mother to find out more about Tommy Gilmour. Our organisation has paid a considerable sum to bring him over to South Africa and
10   we want to get our money's worth. After a long chat I found out lots of interesting things, but the most important fact is that his dad's in prison! Of course, I told his mum that he was doing well here and he was part of the family at St George's. But don't forget, every family has a black sheep.
15   The Gilmour family seems to have at least two!

"I appreciate that, Tommy, I really do. I know that South Africa is not an easy place to live for someone from Europe, but it is a very special country – with very special people. To get on well here, we have to work together. Working to-
20   gether, with honesty, integrity and justice, is the only way we can make South Africa a great country."

I'm not sure which Tommy Gilmour is easier to be with: the one who is cold and sullen and doesn't give a minute of extra time to benefit the school; or the new Tommy who is sitting there, wagging his tail like an obedient puppy who wants to go for a walk.

Well, Tommy, it will give me great pleasure to send you on a long walk – a long walk back to Britain. It was painful to pay all that money to get King to drive you to Kruger for a paid holiday. How many other eighteen-year-olds get an experience like that? We're kind, we're generous and we expect gratitude and hard work. We'll be watching you like a hawk, Tommy Gilmour, and if you do anything wrong, anything at all, you'll be out.

18 January 2020: Soweto, South Africa

Tommy

"Could I have a look at that phone, please?" I asked.

"Which one?" asked the guy in the second-hand phone shop.

"The one with a crack in the screen that looks like a smile."

He took out the phone from under the glass case. "Good phone," he said. "Still working."

I pressed the home button, and sure enough, the phone, my phone, started up. 13% battery, all messages and contacts deleted, but the SIM card still in place.

"How much?"

He quoted a price which made me laugh. *"Angisona isivakashi kuse'khaya la."*

This time he laughed, and the price dropped by more than half. I paid the money and left the shop.

Thank you, Bandile, Amahle's little brother! It was his idea that I check out the second-hand phone shops in Orlando. He knows people that have had their phones stolen three or four times but always get them back a few days later: no contacts, no messages, but the SIM card still there.

With my SIM card still in place, when I turned the phone on, I got messages from my mum, Olivia and Graeme. But the first person I contacted was Amahle. Fortunately I still had the piece of paper with her number on it in my wallet, so I just sent her a quick message.

I'm back.

Seconds later I got a reply.

If it's really you TG, tell me where your father is and your favourite drink.

I understood her concerns and replied.

In prison, mango juice.

Now send me a selfie.

Didn't she believe it was me? Reluctantly I took a selfie and sent it to her.

Don't you believe me?

Back came the reply:

Sure I do. I just wanted to see your happy face. ☺

Good to see that Amahle was smiling. It definitely seemed that my phone was stolen by a couple of amateurs, and we didn't have anything more to worry about – at least about Amahle and Kaya. I still had plenty of worries about Jennifer. That was a weird meeting in her office a few days ago. I told her I was sorry and was going to behave myself. She told me that she appreciated my apology and told me that nonsense about honesty, integrity and justice. I didn't believe a word she said, and she probably didn't believe me either.

One problem is that I don't know who I can trust. It's clear that I can't trust Jennifer at all, but it is probably best if I don't do anything to make her mad at the moment. I would trust Amahle with my life which is a little strange as I've only known her since September, but I don't think there is anyone I trust more than her. So with Jennifer at one end and Amahle at the other, what about the people in the middle? Although they are technically employed by Jennifer, I am confident that Jack and Joe support me. Joe did some great detective work finding out about Patrick Vorster, and Jack and I get on pretty well.

At school I think I can trust Graeme. As far as I know he hasn't told Jennifer anything that I've told him. He could be very useful in the plan that is developing in my head. I'm not sure about Kungawo. He seems to be a good guy and he is Amahle's brother, but he does seem to keep himself to himself. I'm aware that the job he has at St George's is important to him as he supports his family, so it is unlikely that he will want to get involved in my plan. Would he go to Jennifer if I mention the plan to him? I don't think so – but can I risk it? I'm not sure.

Then finally there's Olivia. She's changed a lot – or at least I think she has. She was seriously mad with me when I lied to her about Amahle, and I can understand that. In Kruger, we talked a lot and she can see that Jennifer is a crook;
5 or was she just saying that to get more information about what is going on? I remember at the meal with Jennifer, the two of them got on very well together. I would like to think I can trust Olivia but thinking about it, I'm not so sure. So can I trust them? Graeme, yes. Kungawo, not sure. Olivia,
10 probably not.

Chapter Eighteen

15 January 2020: St George's School,
Johannesburg, South Africa

Graeme

"Jennifer seems to be under a lot of pressure at the moment. Is she okay?" asked Tommy.

"Don't worry about Jennifer. She's a tough cookie."

There's a meeting with the trustees of St George's next week to discuss financial matters, and Jennifer has been working hard preparing for that – but Tommy doesn't need to worry his little head about such things. I have to say it is good to see that Tommy has changed – or at least he *seems* to have changed. Since Christmas he hasn't been late at all and has been throwing himself into his work at St George's. If his change of attitude is genuine, and I still have my doubts, then that is one less thing for Jennifer to worry about. He doesn't need to worry about Jennifer – I'm confident she can look after herself. I had dinner at Jennifer's house last night, and she is definitely a very capable woman.

"Is there anything in particular that's troubling you? You know you can trust me 100%."

He then told me that he knew that Jennifer met Patrick Vorster and that he knew they weren't schoolfriends – so why would she meet him?

"The thing is, Tommy, you probably know the phrase 'it's not what you know, it's who you know'. That is very true in South Africa these days. And we're very lucky that Jennifer knows a lot of people. Without Jennifer's networking skills, St. George's would have closed years ago. I'm sure you know that Patrick Vorster sends his four boys to St. George's. That's a lot of money from one family. I'm sure you under-

5   stand that it is important for Jennifer to stay on good terms with Patrick."

Tommy didn't look convinced.

"That's the truth, Tommy. Other schools in Johannes-burg would love to get Patrick's money, and Jennifer does a

10 great job keeping Patrick happy and his boys at the school."

"So …"

"So what, Tommy?"

"So why did Jennifer give Patrick Vorster an envelope full of cash?"

15 "Are you crazy? Jennifer doesn't deal with cash. You know the school policy on money. It goes in by bank transfer, out by bank transfer. Where did you get such a mad idea from?"

"Oh, someone mentioned it."

"Who?"

20 "I can't remember now."

It was obvious he was lying, but what could I do? Shake the answer out of him? I waited until Tommy had gone off to his lesson, then I legged it to Jennifer's office.

"Tommy knows."

25 "Knows what?"

"About you and Patrick – and the money."

"How would he know something like that?"

"He said someone told him."

"Who?"

30 "He said he couldn't remember."

"This is bad news, Graeme. And I'm disappointed in you that you didn't find out who the troublemaker is."

"I did try, but ..."

"But you didn't get a result, Graeme."

5 Jennifer drummed her fingernails on her desk before continuing. "We're going to have to do something – and pretty quickly."

"Like what?"

"Send Tommy Gilmour back to England – and if he tells
10 the governors of the school about this, then we may have to get out too."

"To England?"

"Sure. That was always the plan, wasn't it?"

15 January 2020: St George's School,
Johannesburg, South Africa

Tommy

"Orlando?"

15 *"Sharp."*

The taxi was pretty packed as we headed out of the Bree taxi rank. I recognised some of my fellow passengers and we nodded our hellos. I was no longer seen as an *umfana wengisi* by most people. I was just a football coach off for
20 some training.

I had arranged to meet Amahle before the session. She wanted to tell me about a match she was planning. But where was she? Amahle's normally never late. I sat in our café with a small coffee and a mango juice.

I was just about to head off to the training ground when a man burst into the café. It was a surprise to see Kungawo in the café and even more of a surprise when he walked over to my table and grabbed me by the front of my shirt.

5 "What have you done with her?"

"I don't know what you mean!"

"Where's Amahle?"

"I don't know. I arranged to meet her here about twenty minutes ago. Maybe she sent me a text."

10 When Kungawo finally let go of my shirt, I took out my phone. There was a message on it.

Leave the country – or Amahle will never walk again.

15 I showed the message to Kungawo. He cried out in anguish and beat his fists on the table.

"The bastards. How could they do this to my wonderful sister?"

I admit I was a bit slow in putting the pieces of the jigsaw 20 together. So it seems Amahle was right; they didn't steal my phone to make money. They did it to prove that she was gay. Amahle had told me about groups of men who want to 'correct' gay women. It was unbearable to think what they might be doing to her.

25 "So, are you going to leave?" asked Kungawo. "I heard Jennifer telling someone that it is time for you to go."

"No way. I can't rest until I know Amahle is safe."

"That's good to hear," said Kungawo. "And I'm sorry that I thought you might be involved in her disappearance."

30 I explained to him about having my phone stolen and getting it back a few days later.

"And you thought they were after your phone?" said Kungawo, shaking his head. "These guys will do anything to carry out their crazy plans."

"So who are these guys? How do we get hold of them?"

"I've no idea. But I am going to do everything to try and find out," said Kungawo. "We've got to work together on this – and we've got to work quickly. You know about Eudy Simelane …"

I did. Amahle had told me about the sad fate of Eudy; a talented football player who was gay. What could we do to save Amahle from the same fate? Kungawo clearly knew more people in Soweto than I did, but when he starts asking around no one will just tell him where she is. We've got to use our brains.

Chapter Nineteen

15 January 2020: Orlando,
Soweto, South Africa

Kungawo

I was pretty relieved to find out that Tommy wasn't involved
in Amahle's disappearance, but I am so angry that some
people think it is okay to just grab a woman off the street
just because she prefers girls, not boys. You hear stories
5 about some men who kidnap gay women. I really hope that
nothing bad happens to my darling sister.

It's going to be tough – no one is going to tell us where
she is. We have to find out for ourselves. There is a small
chance that they will think that because Tommy is white
10 and from England, he must be rich. As a 'rich white' man he
could be willing to pay a kind of ransom to get Amahle
back. If we can get them to start negotiating, then we have
a chance of finding her. As they had sent Tommy a message,
we sent one back.

15 Can we talk?

About a minute later, we got a reply.

No.

Well it was worth a try. What next? Did I know anyone
who might know the people who had taken Amahle? There
20 were a few of the boys I went to school with who had taken

the 'wrong road' and had ended up on the streets. They were the sort of guys who could be persuaded to join a gang. It is very difficult to be respected when you have nothing. Joining a gang is one way that people can get what they see as respect from the community. It is usually the complete opposite – people just don't want trouble, so they steer clear of gang members. Could I get any of my old schoolmates to talk? I doubted it, but I was desperate. I had nothing to lose.

Two nights ago, before Amahle was taken, I took a big risk. I wanted to check out something I heard Olivia and Tommy talking about when we were at the Kruger National Park. Was Jennifer buying up rough diamonds as a good way to get money out of the country? I know one of the cleaners who has a room at St George's. Three days ago, I crept down to her room around midnight. Luckily she was fast asleep, and I was able to slip inside and 'borrow' her school keys for a few minutes. There were about fifteen keys on her bunch. I had no idea which one would open Jennifer's office. If anyone saw me hanging around with a large bunch of keys, then I would almost certainly lose my job. Was it really worth it?

The fifth key I tried opened Jennifer's office. I was immediately struck by the smell of aftershave and I also knew who wore that particular kind of aftershave. But that wasn't important right now. I wanted to know what Jennifer kept in the drawers of her desk. First draw: nothing of interest. Second draw: nothing of interest. Bottom draw: a small blue bag. I picked up the bag carefully and shook the contents onto my hand. There were around 60 rough diamonds.

Olivia

"They've taken Amahle."

It was Tommy.

"Taken her where?" I asked.

"She's been kidnapped – because she's gay."

5 "Shit, Tommy. That's terrible. I know how much she means to you."

I first met Tommy when we had an online meeting on the 5th of November 2018. I was struck then by his attitude – some would say moody, I prefer 'cool'. They say that
10 opposites attract, and I was drawn to Tommy like a moth to a candle. So it was weird to hear him crying on the phone.

"Are you getting support?" I asked. "Have you contacted the police?"

"I suggested it to Kungawo, but he said they wouldn't
15 help us. There's nothing to go on. A girl has gone missing. It happens all the time."

"How do you know she's missing?"

"Kungawo got a call from their mother. She was pretty hysterical. Bandile, their younger brother, saw the kidnap
20 ping but couldn't do anything to stop them."

I took a deep breath and made some calculations in my head. It should work. "Do you remember that café where you introduced me to Amahle?"

"Sure."

25 "I'll see you there at 10 o'clock tomorrow morning. Can you bring Bandile with you?"

"Are you nuts, Olivia? You've got school tomorrow."

"There are things more important than school, Tommy. And friendship is one of them."

Bandile

"Coach Tommy! They took Amahle!"

"I know, Bandile. I'm very sorry. We're going to do every-
5 thing we can to get her back."

"Who's this? Is she your girlfriend?"

"This is Olivia. And no, she's not my girlfriend. She's here to help us find Amahle."

It was strange to be in a café with my brother, Coach
10 Tommy and his friend who isn't his girlfriend. She bought four glasses of mango juice, and we sat in the corner.

"Bandile, can you tell Coach Tommy and Olivia what you told me last night?" said Kungawo. "All about what you saw yesterday."

15 So I told them. I told them how I was kicking a ball around with Desmond in the street. We were practising nutmegging, like Coach Tommy showed us. Desmond is really good at it and nutmegged me three times. Then I saw Amahle, walking towards us. She waved to me. I think she
20 had something for us, so I didn't tell Desmond. I ran past him and ran towards Amahle.

Then I saw a car stop next to Amahle. Three men jumped out. Two of them grabbed Amahle by the arms. I screamed to Desmond. He was playing keepy-uppy. He dropped the
25 ball and ran towards me. I saw Amahle fighting with the two

men. They held her arms, but Amahle kicked one of them where it hurts. The other one slapped her across the face and pushed her to the ground. I was about ten metres away when they threw Amahle into the back of the car. I started banging on the car windows. I could see Amahle's frightened face inside the car. There was nothing I could do to save her. I did try!

Kungawo brushed the tears from my cheeks, and I took a big gulp of mango juice.

"Bandile tried to open the door of the car," said Kungawo. "A man inside kicked him and pulled the door shut."

I showed them the bruise on my leg where the man had kicked me. It still hurt.

"Bandile," said Olivia. "What did the car look like?"

"It was big – and sort of silver – but very dirty."

"And what about the men who grabbed Amahle? What did they look like?" asked Coach Tommy.

"The two men and the driver were all skinny and had dirty hair."

"What about the man in the back of the car?" asked Olivia. "The man who kicked you?"

"He had grey hair and ... and he was wearing a suit."

"Anything else about him?" asked Olivia.

I thought very hard, then I remembered. "He had a tattoo of a lion's head on the back of his hand."

"Thank you, Bandile. You've done a great job," said Olivia and she kissed me on my forehead.

"Are you going to find Amahle now?"

"We're going to do our very very best," she said.

Chapter Twenty

Olivia

Bandile was brilliant – and I can imagine how tough it was for him to see his sister being kidnapped. Now it was our turn to do what we could.

Kungawo clearly knew more people in Soweto than we did, so after taking Bandile home, he went in search of some old school 'friends'. Tommy stayed at the café in the hope that someone would approach him with information. I had a plan of my own – a plan to meet up with a guy that tried to pick me up when I went dancing with Tommy. Fortunately he gave me his card during our brief conversation. It was obvious to me that whatever he did for a living, it wasn't 100% legal. I sent him a text.

> Hi, this is Olivia. I'm the blonde girl from the dance club bar. We met before Christmas. I'm moving to Johannesburg and I'm looking for somewhere to live. Can you help me?

He replied after about ten minutes.

> Sure, I never forget a pretty face. I'll meet you in the same bar where we met. One o'clock?

I couldn't remember where the bar was, but luckily I could message Tommy and ask him. I then contacted Kungawo, and he arranged for a friend to take me there on the back of his motorbike. He would also hang around in case I got into difficulties. My first difficulty was riding on the back of a motorbike – I'd never done it before.

Kungawo

"*Sawubona,* Lubanzi! Remember me? Kungawo! We were at
school together! *Unjani?*"

The answer was clearly not *'sharp'*. Lubanzi lifted his head slowly and stared, not really at me, but through me. It was obvious that he had no idea who I was.

"Lubanzi, do you know about a gang that takes girls that are gay?"

"Beer," said Lubanzi, indicating the empty bottle in front of him.

"I'll get you a beer if you can give me some information. *Sharp?*"

"Beer," said Lubanzi again.

"Do you know a man, probably a gang leader, with a lion tattoo on his hand?"

It seemed that Lubanzi was getting bored of my questions, and instead of repeating 'beer' for a third time, he simply put his head on the table and fell asleep.

There was one other guy who might have some information; a guy called Siyabonga. He used to make money selling fake diamonds to tourists, but then he got in with a bad crowd. It probably wouldn't take too long to find him.

Tommy

"Another mango juice, please."

It was strange sitting in the café, sipping mango juice while Olivia and Kungawo were off doing detective work. I got a message from Kungawo. He found a guy called
5 Lubanzi, but he was no use. He's now going to check out someone called Siyabonga.

I also got a text from Olivia. She has arrived at the dancing club where I took her before Christmas. I don't remember her meeting a guy at the bar, but she showed
10 me his business card.

> Are you sure it's safe to meet him? I can
> come with you if you want.

Her reply came quickly.

> I'll be fine. He'll be happier to talk if it's just me. Kungawo's
15 friend will be outside if there are any problems.

I sent a message to Joe and Jack in Bloemfontein, explaining the situation. Jack wrote back pretty quickly. Jennifer had contacted them, asking if they knew where I was. Someone broke into Jennifer's office, and she is sure
20 that it was me. (It wasn't me, of course.) But it gives Jennifer the excuse she needs to put me on a plane back to England.

I decided to send another message to the kidnappers.

I have money.

Seconds later came the reply.

We are not interested in money.

5   I was just about to order my third mango juice when a girl, about my age, came into the café. She looked around and when she saw me, she started crying.

"Tommy?"

Another piece of the jigsaw fell into place. "Kaya?"

10   She nodded and then hugged me.

"I'm so sorry," I said. "We're doing everything we can to get her back."

"Amahle told me to find you here if anything … happened. She said you're a good person."

15   "Not as good as Amahle," I replied. "But I try my best."

I got a mint tea for Kaya and another mango juice for me, and we sat down to discuss the situation. I showed her the communication with the kidnappers and told her about Kungawo and Olivia. Kaya smiled for the first time.

20   "Amahle told me about the time she first met Olivia. Amahle said Olivia was pretty mad with you."

"She definitely was."

We got back to talking about what we could do to get Amahle back. It was when I mentioned the man with the

25   lion tattoo on his hand that Kaya's eyes widened.

"Do you know him?"

"No, but it is the kind of thing that members of a gang would have. The problem is that there are over one and a half million people in Soweto. There are probably no more than 20 people in the gang."

So how do you find 20 people among 1.5 million? It would be like looking for a needle in a haystack.

"Why don't you get the football players to help you?" suggested Kaya.

"But most of them are young. Some of them are less than ten years old. This could be dangerous."

"These are children from Soweto," said Kaya. "They have grown up with danger all their lives. I'm sure they'll be more than happy to help."

How right she was. I made a quick call to Kungawo who then contacted his brothers and sisters. He called me back about ten minutes later. He reckons around 40 children were now out looking for guys with a lion tattoo on their hand. They had strict instructions not to confront them, but to follow them as carefully as possible.

Chapter Twenty-One

*16 January 2020: Johannesburg,
South Africa*

Olivia

"Innocent?"

"Not me, Oliva. I'm as guilty as they come," laughed Innocent.

I laughed along with him. "Tell me about it."

Amazingly, he did. He told me how he'd grown up in apartheid South Africa, getting a very basic education before leaving school aged 13 to work on the streets. He had done a thousand different jobs, most of them illegal. He was now involved in supplying cheap alcohol to the many bars around Soweto.

I smiled and laughed along with his stories. He was actually quite an entertaining man. But I was here for a purpose.

"So, you know all about me now," said Innocent. "Tell me about you. Why are you moving to Joburg?"

"Actually, Innocent, I've got some bad news for you. I'm not a teacher about to start a new job in Joburg. I work for the South African Revenue Service. I'm doing research on how to cut down on alcohol served in bars around Soweto on which no tax has been paid. We've been looking for people who have been contravening the 2014 Illegal Supply of Alcohol Act. It seems that I've hit the jackpot."

"You're lying," said Innocent. "Why aren't you in some kind of uniform?"

"I don't think you would have told me your life story if you had known who I really was."

I could sense that Innocent was looking for a way out. Would he try and hurt me?

"I have a colleague outside waiting for me if you want to check who I am."

"Okay," said Innocent. "What's your price?"

"My price?"

"Everyone has a price. I'm sure we can strike a deal."

This was my chance. I still had to tread very carefully.

"Well ..."

16 January 2020: Orlando,
Soweto, South Africa

Kungawo

"*Sawubona*, Siyabonga! Remember me? Kungawo. We were at school together."

"Sure, I remember you. What do you want?"

"I don't want anything," I lied. "I was just passing and ..."

"Come on, Kungawo. I know you work at that fancy school in Joburg now. You don't want to hang out with guys like me unless you want something."

It was clear Siyabonga was smarter than I thought. I had to come clean, so I told him about Amahle.

"Your sister's gay?"

"Yes, is that a problem?"

"Well, I suppose not. But she's got to be careful. Tell her to stay away from the Lion Hand Gang. They really hate gay women."

I explained that they had already kidnapped her.

"Shit, man. I'm sorry," said Siyabonga. "The Lion Hand Gang are a dangerous bunch. They deal in drugs and also kidnap gay women."

"Where can I find them?" I asked.

"You really don't want to find them, Kungawo. They kill people and ask questions later."

"I know the risks, but they've got my sister. Please, Siyabonga, help me."

Siyabonga sighed. "You didn't hear any of this from me, right?"

I nodded.

"The Lion Hand Gang control the drugs trade in Orlando and Meadowlands. The leader of the gang is a guy they call The Boss. He lives in a nice house in Diepkloof. You sometimes see him in Orlando, wearing a fancy suit. He looks like a successful businessman, but he's involved in some pretty nasty things."

"Do you know where he lives? Diepkloof is a big area."

"Sorry, Kungawo. I've told you a lot more than I should have. I really hope you get your sister back – alive."

So we're looking for a guy called The Boss who leads the Lion Hand Gang and lives in Diepkloof. Not a lot to go on, but it's a start.

Chapter Twenty-Two

16 January 2020: Orlando,
Soweto, South Africa

Tommy

"So he lives in Diepkloof, wears a suit and is called The Boss."

Kungawo nodded. "It's not much, but we can ask around to see if anyone knows about him – or the Lion Hand Gang."

Kaya and I were still in the café. I was on my fifth mango juice. She had had three mint teas. We had the young footballers coming in to give us regular reports, all of which were negative. The one person I hadn't heard from was Olivia and that was making me a bit nervous.

It was about ten to eight in the evening when Olivia finally returned. I was very happy to see her and filled her in on the information that Kungawo had got from Siyabonga: known as The Boss, lives somewhere in Diepkloof …

"31 Meadowlands Drive," said Olivia. "He's known as The Boss, but his real name is Makazole Nkosi. He's in Cape Town today, but he's flying back to Joburg on the morning flight."

I was impressed. We were all impressed. "How the hell did you find out all that?" I asked.

Olivia smiled. "My friend Innocent told me everything."

It was getting late, but I wanted to check out 31 Meadowlands Drive. Kungawo's friend with the motorbike agreed to take me.

It was starting to get dark as we reached Meadowlands Drive. They were all pretty fancy houses, but number 31 was particularly nice. Window boxes full of geraniums and nicely manicured lawns. Was this really where Amahle was being held? I wanted to shout out to her – let her know that we were coming to save her. But no, better to wait until tomorrow morning. I had a plan slowly forming in my head.

It was almost eleven when I got to bed. Well, some sheets on the floor of Bandile and Desmond's bedroom. Kungawo kindly gave me some of his clothes to wear as I couldn't go back to St George's. Olivia was staying with Kaya. We'd arranged to meet at nine in the morning at the café.

Unable to sleep, I noticed I had two messages. One was from Kaya. She got a message from a girl who had been kidnapped. She had no idea where she was taken, but remembers geraniums in the window boxes and a very tidy garden.

The other message was very short.

You didn't leave. Amahle will not walk again.

17 January 2020: O.R. Tambo International
Airport, Johannesburg, South Africa

Makazole Nkosi, aka The Boss

"Have a nice day, sir," said the stewardess as I left the plane.

"Thank you."

I walked through the VIP lounge at the airport, enjoyed a quick latte, then met my driver outside.

"Good morning, Mandla. All good?"

"Yes, sir. All very good, sir."

"Is the girl safe?"

"Yes, sir. Very safe."

"Any news about the English boy?"

5 "He was in the café all day, sir. He was with the girl's ... friend, sir."

Strange. I expected more from the boy. I got his pathetic little text messages. Did he really think that I would negotiate with him? He even offered me money. What a joke. I
10 earn more in a day than Tommy cracked-phone Gilmour earns in a year.

I had to read all the messages on his phone. He has very strong feelings for the girl. It's a shame she didn't have the same feelings for him, or she wouldn't be in the mess she's
15 in now. Of course, it is the girl that needs correcting, but I like to play mind games with the people that support such girls – and it really isn't difficult to mess up a little mind like Tommy Gilmour's.

Of course, this whole thing is the government's fault.
20 We're still the only country in Africa that allows two men or two women to get married. What is wrong with these people? It's clear they have to be stopped! As the government won't stop them – it is up to responsible citizens like me to show them the correct way.

25 "Mandla, did you get the hammers I asked for?"

"Yes, sir. One large, one small hammer, sir."

"Very good."

As this girl is so keen on football, it is time for her to have a break – literally, so that she can think about her life choices.
30 We are giving her the chance to realise how much better it

is to be with a man. Let's hope that she realises the mistakes she has made.

"Mandla, who are all those kids in the minibuses? Is there a football game in Diepkloof today?"

"Not that I'm aware of, sir. But I'll find out, sir. Let's get you home first, sir."

I don't like being unaware of things. I pay good money to the gang so that they can inform me of what is going on. Mandla parked my car in the garage and then carried the hammers into the house. Now I had to get to work.

17 January 2020: Diepkloof,
Soweto, South Africa

Tommy

"Did you get it?"

"Yep," said Joe, checking the back of his camera. "Two hammers: one big, one small."

I thought of the text: Amahle will not walk again. That's why the bastard had two hammers.

"Okay, guys! Let's go!"

I have to say it was Olivia's idea. Bring as many football players to the area as possible and get them to kick as many balls around as they can, and the whole street calls the police to complain, and in a rich area like this, the police actually do turn up pretty quickly. There were players that I trained, that Amahle trained and others from other parts of Soweto – even from Diepkloof. From inside the minibus, we watched as they ran up and down Meadowlands Drive, kicking balls against gates and windows, shouting and singing.

It took about five minutes before we saw the first police car. After ten minutes there were five of them. The poor police officers were not sure how to deal with over one hundred football players kicking balls around the street. But would they listen to us if we told them about Amahle and The Boss?

"Open up!" A police officer banged on the side of our minibus. She did not look happy at all.

"Are you responsible for all these kids causing mayhem?"

"Well ..." I began.

"Yes, I'm afraid we are, officer," said Olivia. "But there's a good reason for it."

"This had better be good," said the officer as a football bashed against the side of the minibus, narrowly missing her head.

Olivia was brilliant. She showed them the texts from The Boss and also the photos that Jack took of the hammers.

"Okay, I need to call my boss. We can't just go charging into someone's house."

"Not even when a crime is about to be committed?" I asked. "My friend here is a student journalist and he's making a documentary about police in South Africa and what a great job they're doing."

She looked at Joe with his video camera. Joe waved back. "Well we are doing our best ..."

Chapter Twenty-Three

17 January 2020: 31 Meadowlands Drive,
Diepkloof, Soweto, South Africa

Amahle

"You look just as disgusting as you really are," he said.

"My body is dirty, but my mind is pure," I replied.

"Pure? You think your mind is pure? Your mind is a sewer. Your mind is corrupted. Your mind is deranged."

5 He was pacing around the room with a hammer in his hand. It seemed that I wasn't going to leave the room alive.

"There is a disease in this country, and it has to be stopped. A disease that affects the brains of young women. It makes them think that ..."

10 He paused and went to the window. We could both hear a lot of shouting. I heard someone shout, *"Ngiyingane enkulu!"* It wasn't Tommy, but it was definitely one of Tommy's boys.

Seconds later a football hit the window.

15 "What the ..."

The man grabbed his phone. "Get over here, now! What do you mean, you can't? No one disobeys The Boss ... I'll deal with you later."

He took a small gun from inside his jacket, smashed the
20 glass and started firing out of the window. I heard screams from the street, but the man kept on firing.

"STOP IT!" I shouted as loud as I could. "Shoot at me, not the children!"

He did stop. Then he slowly moved his gun until it was pointing directly at my head. I closed my eyes and thought of my mother, my father, my brothers and sisters, Kaya and Tommy.

Then came the shattering of glass and a large cry. I opened my eyes to see the man clutch his heart and stagger backwards against the table. His smart white suit was quickly turning bright red. He looked at me one last time before collapsing on the floor.

17 January 2020: Diepkloof police station,
Soweto, South Africa

Tommy

"She's asking for Kaya and Tommy," said the police officer.

"Thank you," I said. "Thank you for everything."

The police officer smiled as she opened the door to the police interview room.

I had never seen Amahle cry before, but when she saw us the floodgates opened. "I love you both so much."

That, of course, made Kaya and me cry as well, but we didn't care. We had our Amahle back again.

Chapter Twenty-Four

24 January 2020: Bond Street,
London, England

Christopher Hutton (jeweller)

"Can I help you, madam?"

"I certainly hope so. My South African grandmother died recently and left me a small bag of rough diamonds. Frankly I have no idea what they're worth, but I would welcome your expert opinion."

"May I take a look at the diamonds, madam?"

"Graeme, you've got them in your bag," said the woman with the strong South African accent.

Before I even saw the diamonds, I was pretty sure what I was going to see. I've been in the business for over 40 years and I get about five people every year coming to me, trying to sell what they think are rough diamonds, but in fact are pieces of shiny glass. I've actually been to Vilakazi Street in Soweto where some very clever hustlers convince tourists that they have some rough diamonds that their uncle, father or grandfather smuggled out of one of the big mines. The tourists return home thinking they are going to be rich and then are horribly disappointed to find that their 'rough diamonds' are worthless.

She took out a small blue bag and handed it to me. As a true professional, I picked up my loupe and took out one of the diamonds with a pair of tweezers. It was quite a nice piece of glass, but definitely glass, not a diamond. I took out a few more of the stones but all with the same result.

"So, how much are they worth?" said the South African woman.

5   "I'm afraid these are not diamonds, madam. These are pieces of glass."

"What? Are you nuts? I paid 250,000 dollars for these!"

It was interesting that she had paid a quarter of a million dollars for some pieces of glass, yet she was accusing me of

10 being nuts. Also interesting that her story had changed from the diamonds being from her grandmother to having paid *a lot* of money for them.

"This is all your fault, Graeme. I told you to get them checked."

15 "I *did* get them checked," said her companion. "The jeweller in Joburg told me they were real."

"So why does this buffoon tell me they're not?"

"I don't know. Perhaps Patrick Vorster tricked us somehow. He was in prison for a while."

20 "He wouldn't do that. He ..."

It was at this moment that the woman started sobbing loudly and was led out of the shop by a security guard and onto a cold and miserable Bond Street.

Chapter Twenty-Five

1 March 2020: St George's School,
Johannesburg, South Africa

Tommy

Dear Manni,

Quite a bit to tell you about what has happened since we rescued Amahle from the Lion Hand Gang. I was really impressed with Olivia and the work that she did. Not only
5 did she get the address of The Boss, she also contacted Jack and Joe to come and help on the 17th of January. Kaya was brilliant, organising all the young football players. It seems she has contacts all over Soweto.

Kungawo finally told us the full story of Jennifer's
10 office. Apparently he heard me and Olivia discussing Jennifer when we were in the Kruger National Park. Back at St George's, he 'borrowed' a key from the cleaner and broke into Jennifer's office. He found a small blue bag full of uncut diamonds in one of her drawers. The next day, he went to
15 Vilakazi Street and bought some fake diamonds from an old friend. Then he broke into Jennifer's office a second time – the night before Amahle was kidnapped. This time, he replaced the real diamonds with the fake ones. Unfortunately, he knocked over a vase of flowers while he was there
20 which is how Jennifer knew someone had been in her office. After getting back to his room, Kungawo contacted the trustees of the school, explaining what he had found out and telling them about Joe's video work with the money and the picture of Patrick Vorster and Jennifer.

The trustees called Jennifer to an extraordinary meeting, but she never showed up. She and Graeme Logan disappeared, and the police told us they had flown to London. The police were able to access Jennifer's emails which showed that Jennifer had been accepting cash or rough diamonds from rich families for years – saving them up as part of her 'retirement package'.

We haven't heard from them since, but I hear they did take the small bag of shiny stones that Kungawo left in her drawer. I wonder if honesty, integrity and justice will be part of their future lives. Somehow I doubt it.

The trustees were very happy to get the real diamonds from Kungawo and were able to sell them for a large sum of money. (They won't say how much.) They set up a special fund with the money – money to be used to help a variety of educational projects.

I am happy to say that one of the projects is a joint football coaching project with Orlando and St George's.

I'm sure you want to know what happened to Amahle. Well, the trustees agreed to fund Amahle to work as a teacher at St Clothild's, a girls' school not far from St George's. But she can also train the girls in Orlando.

I went to see her last night. She's just moved into a little flat near her school. She is happier than I've ever seen her before, and I am pretty sure she's got a great future ahead of her.

One final thing. At the beginning of January, Amahle mentioned that she was planning a football match for the boys I train, but she said it was a work in progress. I can now tell you that she was planning a match against St George's. Well, we finally played the match last week.

The MangoBoys (as Amahle called them) played St George's Under Thirteens (Graeme's old team). I am happy to report that the MangoBoys thrashed St George's 7–1.

Vocabulary

Abbreviations

sb. = somebody; sth. = something;
Abk. = Abkürzung; etw. = etwas; jmdm. = jemandem; jmdn. = jemanden;
umg. = umgangssprachlich

A

accountancy [əˈkaʊntənsi]
   Buchhaltung; Rechnungs-
   wesen

(to) **accuse** sb. [əˈkjuːz]
   jmdn. beschuldigen

(to) **adore** sb. [əˈdɔː]
   jmdn. bewundern

(to) **affect** sth. [əˈfekt]
   sich auf etw. auswirken

airhead [ˈeəhed]   *umg.* Hohlkopf

alive [əˈlaɪv]   lebend

amount [əˈmaʊnt]   Menge

anger [ˈæŋɡə]   Wut

(to) **apologise** [əˈpɒlədʒaɪz]
   sich entschuldigen

apparantly [əˈpærəntli]
   anscheinend

(to) **appreciate** sb./sth.
   [əˈpriːʃieɪt]   jmdn./etw.
   schätzen

apprenticeship [əˈprentɪʃɪp]
   Ausbildung, Lehre

ashamed [əˈʃeɪmd]**:** (to) **be
   ashamed**   sich schämen

attentively [əˈtentɪvli]
   aufmerksam

(to) **avoid** sth. [əˈvɔɪd]
   etw. vermeiden

aware [əˈweə]**:** (to) **be aware**
   sich bewusst sein

awkward [ˈɔːkwəd]   peinlich

B

(to) **backpack** [ˈbækpæk]
   nur mit Rucksack reisen

(to) **bang** [bæŋ]   schlagen

barely [ˈbeəli]   kaum

the **basics** [ˈbeɪsɪks]
   die Grundlagen

beaming [biːmɪŋ]   strahlend

behaviour [bɪˈheɪvjə]   Benehmen

belief [bɪˈliːf]   *hier:* Überzeugung

bench [bentʃ]   Bank *(zum Sitzen)*

(to) **benefit** [ˈbenɪfɪt]   profitieren

(to) **bet** [bet]   wetten

blink [blɪŋk]   Zwinkern
   in the blink of an eye
   blitzschnell

boerewors [ˈbuːrəvɔːs]
südafrikanische Wurstspeziali-
tät aus mehreren Sorten
Fleisch, die in Schneckenform
gerollt und kräftig gewürzt ist

(to) **bother** [ˈbɒðə]
sich die Mühe machen

bright [braɪt]   *hier:* intelligent

bubble [ˈbʌbl]   Blase

bucket [ˈbʌkɪt]   Eimer

buffoon [bəˈfuːn]   *veraltet* Clown

bullet [ˈbʊlɪt]   Kugel
(Schusswaffe)

C

(to) **chain** sb. [tʃeɪn]   jmdn.
anketten

cheeky [ˈtʃiːki]   frech

chest [tʃest]   Brust

clue [kluː]   Ahnung

(to) **clutch** sth. [klʌtʃ]
etw. umklammern

(to) **collapse** [kəˈlæps]
zusammenbrechen

(to) **commit** [kəˈmɪt]
sich verpflichten
(to) **commit a crime**
eine Straftat begehen

commitment [kəˈmɪtmənt]
Engagement

concern [kənˈsɜːn]   Bedenken

(to) **confess** [kənˈfes]   gestehen

confidence [ˈkɒnfɪdəns]
Zuversicht; Vertrauen

(to) **consider** [kənˈsɪdə]
in Erwägung ziehen

(to) **contravene** sth. [ˌkɒntrəˈviːn]
gegen etw. verstoßen

convinced [kənˈvɪnst]   überzeugt

cookie [ˈkʊki]: **tough cookie**
umg. zäher Typ

(to) **cope** [kəʊp]   gewachsen sein

courage [ˈkʌrɪdʒ]   Mut

crack [kræk]   *hier:* großer Kratzer

crossbar [ˈkrɒsbɑː]   Querlatte

curious [ˈkjʊəriəs]   neugierig

curling [ˈkɜːlɪŋ]: **curling free kick**
angeschnittener Freistoß

D

deaf [def]   schwerhörig

death [deθ]   Tod

(to) **dedicate** [ˈdedɪkeɪt]:
(to) **dedicate oneself to** sth.
sich etw. widmen

dedicated [ˈdedɪkeɪtɪd]
engagiert

dedication [ˌdedɪˈkeɪʃn]   Hingabe

(to) **defend** sb./sth. [dɪˈfend]
jmdn./etw. verteidigen

defender [dɪˈfendə]   Verteidiger(in)

deranged [dɪˈreɪndʒd]   gestört

desire [dɪˈzaɪə]   *hier:* Wunsch

desirable [dɪˈzaɪərəbl]   begehrt

desperate [ˈdespərət]
verzweifelt

determined [dɪˈtɜːmɪnd]
entschlossen

devastated [ˈdevəsteɪtɪd]
erschüttert

digestion [daɪˈdʒestʃən]
Verdauung

disappearance [ˌdɪsəˈpɪərəns]
Verschwinden

(to) **disobey** sb. [ˌdɪsəˈbeɪ]
jmdm. nicht gehorchen

distraction [dɪˈstrækʃn]
Ablenkung

doubt [daʊt] Zweifel

dust [dʌst] Staub

Dutch [dʌtʃ]: (to) **go Dutch**
getrennt bezahlen

E

edible [ˈedəbl] essbar

EDM [ˌiː diː ˈem] *Abk.* elektro-
nische Tanzmusik *(electronic dance music)*

educational [ˌedʒuˈkeɪʃənl]
Bildungs-

effort [ˈefət] Mühe

empathy [ˈempəθi] Einfühlungs-
vermögen

employed [ɪmˈplɔɪd] angestellt,
beschäftigt

employer [ɪmˈplɔɪə] Arbeit-
geber(in)

encouragement [ɪnˈkʌrɪdʒmənt]
Anfeuerung; Unterstützung

(to) **engage** sb. in sth. [ɪnˈgeɪdʒ]
jmdn. in etw. verwickeln

entirely [ɪnˈtaɪəli] völlig

envelope [ˈenvələʊp] Umschlag

evidence [ˈevɪdəns] Beweisstück

expenses [ɪkˈspensiːz] Unkosten

extraordinary [ɪkˈstrɔːdnri]
außerordentlich

F

fake [feɪk] falsch; gefälscht

favour [ˈfeɪvə] Gefallen

fellow [ˈfeləʊ] *umg.* Kerl

five-a-side [ˌfaɪv ə ˈsaɪd] *fünf Spieler(innen) pro Mannschaft*

flavour [ˈfleɪvə] Geschmack

floodgate [ˈflʌdgeɪt]
Schleusentor

fond [fɒnd]: (to) **be fond of** sb./
sth. jmdn./etw. gern mögen

fund [fʌnd] Fonds

fuss [fʌs] Aufregung

G

generous [ˈdʒenərəs] großzügig

genuine [ˈdʒenjuɪn] echt
genuinely *hier:* wirklich

goal [gəʊl] Tor *(Fußball)*
(to) **score a goal** ein Tor
schießen

granny [ˈgræni] Oma

grateful [ˈgreɪtfl] dankbar

gratitude [ˈgrætɪtjuːd]
Dankbarkeit

gravy [ˈgreɪvi] (Braten-)Soße

growth mindset
[ˌgrəʊθ ˈmaɪndset] *die Überzeugung, aus allen Situationen etwas zu lernen und sich dadurch weiter zu entwickeln*

guilty [ˈgɪlti] schuldig

gut [gʌt] Darm

gymnasium [dʒɪmˈneɪziəm]
Turnhalle

H

habitat [ˈhæbɪtæt] Lebensraum
hawk [hɔːk] Falke
haystack [ˈheɪstæk] Heuhaufen
hell [hel] Hölle
hesitation [ˌhezɪˈteɪʃn] *hier:*
    Bedenken
hilarious [hɪˈleəriəs] urkomisch
honesty [ˈɒnəsti] Ehrlichkeit
hugger [hʌgə] *umg. jemand, der*
    gern Leute umarmt
hustler [ˈhʌslə] Betrüger(in)

I

impassively [ɪmˈpæsɪvli]
    unbeeindruckt
impressive [ɪmˈpresɪv]
    beeindruckend
induced coma [ɪnˈdjuːst ˌkəʊmə]
    künstliches Koma
induction [ɪnˈdʌkʃn]
    (Amts-)Einführung
injustice [ɪnˈdʒʌstɪs]
    Ungerechtigkeit
(to) **insult** sb. [ˈɪnsʌlt] jmdn.
    beleidigen
integrity [ɪnˈtegrəti] Integrität
(to) **intimidate** sb. [ɪnˈtɪmɪdeɪt]
    jmdn. einschüchtern

J

joy [dʒɔɪ] Freude
justice [ˈdʒʌstɪs] Gerechtigkeit

K

kerb [kɜːb] Bordstein
(to) **kidnap** sb. [ˈkɪdnæp]
    jmdn. entführen
knowledgeable [ˈnɒlɪdʒəbl]
    sachkundig
kota [ˈkəʊtə] *südafrikanisches*
    Sandwich

L

lack [læk] Mangel
laughter [ˈlɑːftə] Lachen
lawn [lɔːn] Rasen
liar [ˈlaɪə] Lügner(in)
lioness [ˈlaɪənes] Löwin
loo [luː] *umg.* Klo
loupe [luːp] Lupe
    (von Juwelieren)

M

(to) **maintain** sth. [meɪnˈteɪn]
    etw. behalten
maize [meɪz] Mais
mayhem [ˈmeɪhem] Chaos
mine [maɪn] Mine *(Bergwerk)*
moth [mɒθ] Motte
mould [məʊld] Schimmel
(to) **munch** [mʌntʃ] futtern;
    mampfen

N

nasty [ˈnɑːsti] schlimm
(to) **negotiate** [nɪˈgəʊʃieɪt]
    verhandeln
niece [niːs] Nichte

(to) **nutmeg** sb. [ˈnʌtmeg]
den Ball durch die Beine
des Gegners spielen

nutritional scientist
[njuˈtrɪʃənl ˈsaɪəntɪst]
Ernährungswissen-
schaftler(in)

O

obedient [əˈbiːdiənt] folgsam
obvious [ˈɒbviəs] offensichtlich
occasion [əˈkeɪʒn] Gelegenheit
occasionally [əˈkeɪʒnəli]
gelegentlich
offensive [əˈfensɪv] anstößig;
unverschämt
offside [ˌɒfˈsaɪd] abseits
offside trap [ˈɒfsaɪd træp]
Abseitsfalle
opponent [əˈpəʊnənt]
Gegner(in)
oppressive [əˈpresɪv]
unterdrückerisch
outlet [ˈaʊtlet] *hier:* Ventil

P

pace [peɪs]**:** (to) **put sb. through
their paces** jmdn. auf Herz
und Nieren prüfen
pain [peɪn]**:** (to) **be a pain in
the neck** *umg.* nerven
particularly [pəˈtɪkjələli]
besonders

passionate [ˈpæʃənət]**:** (to) **be
passionate about** sth.
sich für etw. brennend
interessieren
(to) **pat** [pæt] tätscheln
pathetic [pəˈθetɪk] *abwertend*
lächerlich
(to) **peel** [piːl] schälen
peester [ˈpiːstə] *Schimpfwort*
Pimmel
penalty [ˈpenəlti] Elfmeter
penalty area Strafraum
PhD [ˌpiː eɪtʃ ˈdiː] *akademischer
Grad (entspricht dem Doktor-
titel)*
pitch [pɪtʃ] Spielfeld
plain [pleɪn] Ebene
posh [pɒʃ] vornehm
potted [ˈpɒtɪd] gekürzt;
in Kurzform
(to) **pour** [pɔː] gießen
predator [ˈpredətə] Raubtier
(to) **presume** [prɪˈzjuːm]
annehmen, vemuten
proof [pruːf] Beweis
prospective [prəˈspektɪv] *hier:*
potenziell
puddle [ˈpʌdl] Pfütze
(to) **puke** sth. up [pjuːk] *umg.*
etw. auskotzen
purpose [ˈpɜːpəs] Zweck

R

rand [rænd] Rand *(Währungs-
einheit in Südafrika)*
range [reɪndʒ] Spektrum
ransom [ˈrænsəm] Lösegeld

(to) **rattle** sb. [ˈrætl] *umg.* jmdn. aus dem Konzept bringen

(to) **reckon** [ˈrekən] glauben, meinen

(to) **recognise** [ˈrekəgnaɪz] erkennen

referee [refəˈriː] Schiedsrichter(in)

relieved [rɪˈliːvd] erleichtert

reluctantly [rɪˈlʌktəntli] widerwillig

(to) **rely** on sb./sth. [rɪˈlaɪ] sich auf etw./jmdn. verlassen; auf etw./jmdn. angewiesen sein

(to) **remain** [rɪˈmeɪn] bleiben

replacement [rɪˈpleɪsmənt] Ersatz

research [rɪˈsɜːtʃ] Forschung

retired [rɪˈtaɪəd] im Ruhestand

rope [rəʊp] Seil
    (to) **show sb. the ropes** jmdn. in etw. einweisen

rough [rʌf] Roh-

(to) **rule** [ruːl] herrschen; bestimmen

S

sake [seɪk]: **for the sake of** sth. um einer Sache willen

saliva [səˈlaɪvə] Speichel

samp [sæmp] *eine Art Brei aus gestampften Maiskörnern*

satnav [ˈsætnæv] *umg.* Navi

(to) **scamper** [ˈskæmpə] *umg.* flitzen

scholarship [ˈskɒləʃɪp] Stipendium

sewer [ˈsuːə] Kloake

shamelessly [ˈʃeɪmləsli] schamlos

shape [ʃeɪp] Form

shopkeeper [ˈʃɒpkiːpə] Ladeninhaber(in)

sincere [sɪnˈsɪə] aufrichtig; ehrlich

sixth form [ˈsɪksθ fɔːm] *die beiden letzten Schuljahre vor dem A level*

(to) **snatch** [snætʃ] schnappen

(to) **sob** [sɒb] schluchzen

sombre [ˈsɒmbə] düster; ernst

splendid [ˈsplendɪd] *veraltet* großartig

squad [skwɒd] Mannschaft

(to) **squeeze** [skwiːz] drücken

(to) **stagger** [ˈstægə] wanken

standpipe [ˈstændpaɪp] Steigrohr

(to) **steer** [stɪə]: (to) **steer clear of** sb./sth. sich von jmdm./etw. fernhalten

(to) **strike** [straɪk]: (to) **strike a deal** sich auf etw. einigen

stubbornness [ˈstʌbənnəs] Sturheit

stunning [ˈstʌnɪŋ] umwerfend

suspicion [səˈspɪʃn] Verdacht

T

tangent [ˈtændʒənt]: (to) **go off on a tangent** *umg.* vom Thema abkommen

taxi rank [ˈtæksi ræŋk] Taxistand

thought [θɔːt] Gedanke

thrilled [θrɪld]: (to) **be thrilled**
vor Freude außer sich sein

tinted [ˈtɪntɪd] getönt

touchline [ˈtʌtʃlaɪn] Seitenlinie

trail mix [ˈtreɪl mɪks]
Studentenfutter

transfer [ˈtrænsfɜ:]: **bank
transfer** Überweisung

(to) **tread** [tred]: (to) **tread
carefully** vorsichtig
vorgehen

(to) **treat** sb. [tri:t] jmdn.
behandeln

trustee [trʌˈsti:] *hier: Mitglied
der Schulstiftung*

tweezers [ˈtwi:zəz] Pinzette

U

unaware [ˌʌnəˈweə]: (to) **be
unaware** nicht bemerken

unbearable [ʌnˈbeərəbl]
unerträglich

unconditional [ˌʌnkənˈdɪʃənl]
vorbehaltlos

undoubtedly [ʌnˈdaʊtɪdli]
zweifellos

unsavoury [ʌnˈseɪvəri]
widerlich; zweifelhaft

upfield [ˌʌpˈfi:ld] (nach) vorn

uprising [ˈʌpraɪzɪŋ] Aufstand

upset [ˌʌpˈset] aufgebracht

urgently [ˈɜ:dʒəntli] dringend

V

vaccination [ˌvæksɪˈneɪʃn]
Impfung

variety [vəˈraɪəti] Vielzahl

various [ˈveəriəs] verschieden

(to) **vow** sth. [vaʊ] etw.
geloben; *hier auch:* sich etw.
vornehmen

W

wand [wɒnd] Zauberstab

weird [wɪəd] *hier:* merkwürdig

willing [ˈwɪlɪŋ] bereit

windscreen [ˈwɪndskri:n]
Windschutzscheibe

worthless [ˈwɜ:θləs] wertlos

Zulu phrases from the book

Angisona isivakashi kuse'khaya la.
I'm not a visitor – I live here.

ayikho inkinga
no problem

Ngidinga ukunya.
I need a shit.

Ngidinga ukunya ngokushesha.
I need a shit urgently.

ngiyabonga
thank you

Ngiyingane enkulu.
I'm a big baby.

sawubona
hello

sharp
good; you're welcome

sho
you're welcome; yes

umfana wengisi
white boy

Unjani?
How are you?

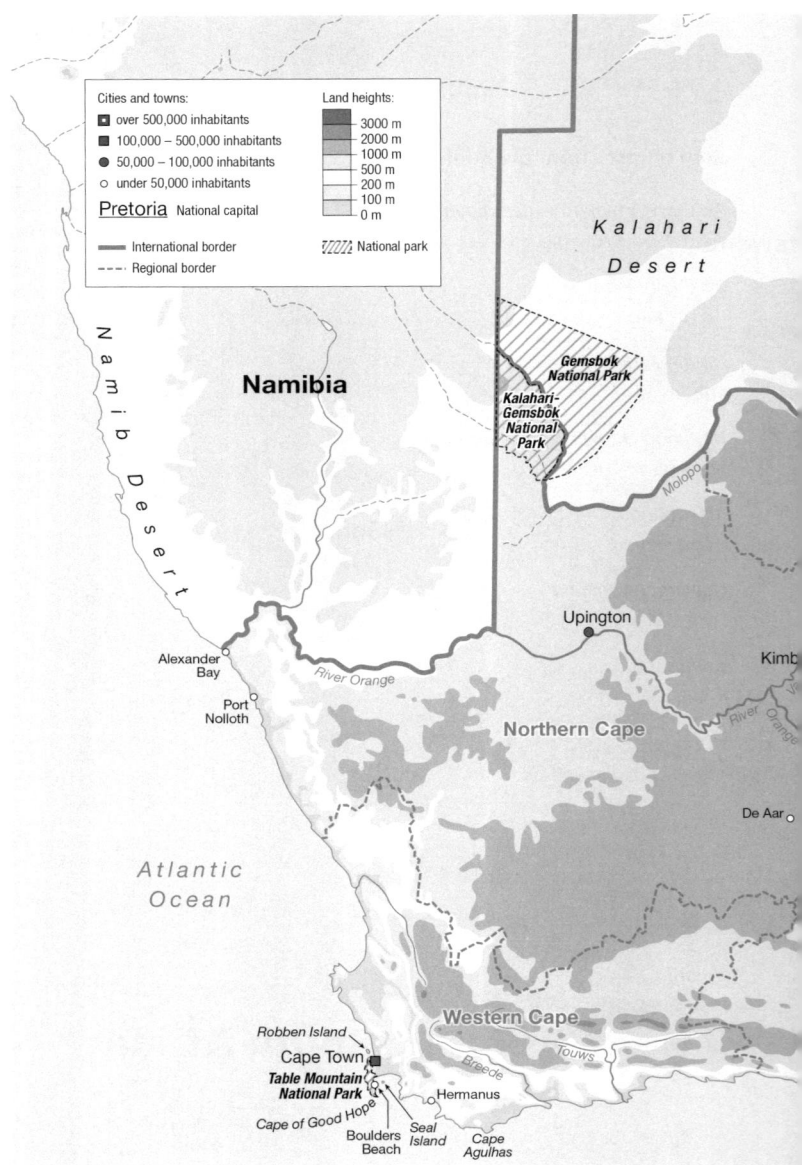

Cities and towns:
- ⊡ over 500,000 inhabitants
- ■ 100,000 – 500,000 inhabitants
- ● 50,000 – 100,000 inhabitants
- ○ under 50,000 inhabitants

<u>Pretoria</u> National capital

━━━ International border
--- Regional border

Land heights:
- 3000 m
- 2000 m
- 1000 m
- 500 m
- 200 m
- 100 m
- 0 m

▨ National park

Kalahari

Desert

N
a
m
i
b

D
e
s
e
r
t

Namibia

Gemsbok National Park

Kalahari-Gemsbok National Park

Molopo

Upington ●

Kimb

River Orange

Alexander ○
Bay

Port ○
Nolloth

Northern Cape

De Aar ○

River Orange

Atlantic Ocean

Western Cape

Robben Island

Cape Town ■

Table Mountain National Park

Cape of Good Hope

Boulders Beach

Seal Island

Cape Agulhas

Hermanus ○

Breede

Touws

Francistown

Zimbabwe

Gonarezhou
National
Park

GREAT

LIMPOPO

Zinave
National
Park

Banhine
National
Park

TRANSFRONTIER

PARK

Limpopo
National
Park

tswana

Limpopo

Kruger

Mozambique

Polokwane

Phalaborwa

aborone

Lepelle

Limpopo

National

Sun
City

Park

<u>Pretoria</u>

ahikeng
nabatho

Krugersdorp

Mbombela

Gauteng

Mpumalanga

Maputo

Johannesburg

<u>Mbabane</u>

North West

Sharpeville

Swazi-
land

Vaal

Welkom

Vaal

Free State

Kwazulu-
Natal

Tugela

mfontein

<u>Maseru</u>

Pietermaritz-
burg

Eswatini

to
Eastern
Cape

Durban

Caledon

Kokstad

River Orange

Mthatha
(Umtata)

Indian
Ocean

stern Cape

Gr. Fish

East
London

South Africa

rt
zabeth

| 0 | | 50 | | 100 | | 150 miles |
| 0 | 50 | 100 | 150 | 200 | 250 kilometres |